INV

HOW TO BE SUCCESSFUL AS A FRANCHISEE

DOUG DOWNER

ISBN: 978-8-26931-666-7
ISBN: 978-8-26931-667-4

CONTENTS

LIST OF FIGURES

PREFACE

Have you heard that 90% of all businesses fail? Or that 50% of new businesses fail? Read enough articles on the subject, and you'll likely read or hear a wide spectrum of claims, mostly falling between these two extremes.

AdvisorSmith found that 22% of small businesses fail within the first year, 32% fail within the first two years and 40% fail within the first three years of business. Half of small businesses fail within the first five years, and two-thirds (66%) fail within ten years.

Whatever the number, that's scary!

Not everyone can or should become a business owner. Statistically, around 16% of the world's eligible working population get into business ownership, and they do this for several reasons: to be their own boss, to take control of their life and future, the pride of being a business owner and hopefully to be more financial and successful than remaining in paid employment. It is estimated that business owners generate an income that is 30% higher than had they stayed in employment.

Every time I walk past an empty shop, my stomach twists in knots because that means somebody's dream and potentially their livelihood has been impacted in a negative way. No one goes into business thinking it's not going to work, but the statistics show an alarming failure rate for small businesses.

This is why I love franchising. Whilst it's not a guarantee of success, the statistics are significantly more positive than for independent businesses.

But just like the statement above regarding overall business success, you'll hear a range of statistics relating to franchise success rates, globally ranging between 80–90% success rate. This may be a little deceptive, however, as some franchisees may not be able to make a particular location work, but another operator may. In a lot of cases, particularly where the franchisor holds the head lease, the franchisor may take over the operation or sell that business to another franchisee. I don't say that to alarm anyone, but it's a reality. Some people just aren't right for business or particular businesses and the stage of that particular brand's growth, and there are so many factors that influence the success of a business. But it is widely known that franchised businesses have a far greater success rate than independent businesses.

Why Did I Call the Book *INVESTED*?

Before I explain my rationale for the book title, we need to understand the dictionary definition of investment: *it is the action or process of investing money for profit or material result.*

An investment is an asset or item acquired with the goal of generating income or appreciation. Appreciation refers to an increase in the value of an asset over time.

An investment always concerns the outlay of some resource today — time, effort, money, or an asset — in hopes of a greater payoff in the future than what was originally put in.

Because investing is oriented toward the potential for future growth or income, there is always a certain level of risk associated with an investment. An investment may not generate the desired level of income or may actually lose value over time.

Now that we know the basic principles of investment, why did I title this book *Invested*?

Well, to start with, going into franchising meets all of the definitions associated with the textbook explanation of investment, but it goes way deeper than that, and it is important that anyone considering investing in a business understands the risks associated with their investment.

There are three key perspectives that I want to relate to 'investment' as it pertains to franchising. Firstly, my commitment, participation, ownership and experience in the franchise sector positions me as an authority on franchising and enables me to be in a position to write this book for the benefit of potential franchisees. Secondly, the potential franchisee and their investment in time, money and commitment to the business they buy into. Thirdly, the franchisor and their investment in the development of the franchise model and the ongoing support that they provide to their franchisees.

There are many books written about franchising, and some of them are actually very well written and written by people that have the expertise to share. If I draw parallels between business and sport, you will know that often the best coaches weren't necessarily the best players in their chosen sport but go on to greatness, and I am sure this is true of business coaches and franchise consultants.

I am a little dubious of the latter, but I am sure there are great business coaches that have never owned and operated a business and franchise consultants that have never owned a franchise business themselves. However, I truly believe that in order to give the best advice, an individual needs to have had some personal experience in the area they are consulting in. I share this thought process with you so that I can share my credentials for writing this book. Not everything I have been involved in has been the success that I thought it would be, but I will share my learnings from those experiences later in the book.

I have worked my whole life in the franchise sector, starting with what I consider the best franchise system in the world — McDonald's. I started my franchise career back in 1983 and spent 14 years with McDonald's, operating at most management and middle management levels within the organisation, but it was my national training and development role in the last three years with McDonald's that prepared me for a life of developing franchise systems.

I left McDonald's and then worked in seven other franchise brands as either director, CEO or general manager, helping each of those brands grow significantly. This experience was in hospitality, retail and professional services.

After a successful career as an employee within the franchise sector, I knew that I wanted to own and operate my own businesses, and during my fulltime employment career, I owned two franchises as a franchisee.

In 2014, I purchased the Australian rights to a master franchise from the USA, called The Alternative Board, a business coaching franchise. This business grew to 20 business coaches, and in 2019, I sold the master franchise to an existing franchisee in the network because I had niched into the franchise sector with my coaching, advisory and consulting services.

I had been doing franchise consulting work since 2008, but as a side hustle to my main roles and businesses that I was involved in. I would assist between 3–4 businesses each year, scale and grow through franchising through a consultancy service that I offered.

In 2019, I went all in, sold The Alternative Board business and set about establishing the best franchise consulting business in Australia — Franchise Ready. We started to recruit a team to assist with the growth of our business and the clients that we work with.

Franchise Ready have helped launch and support hundreds of brands by early 2023 and on average will assist 45–50 new brands enter franchising each year and another 50 existing franchise brands take their businesses to the next level through the consulting services we offer. We are a full-service franchise development and consulting business that can help businesses to scale and grow through franchising.

When you work closely with business owners, you obtain a deep insight into a business and see significant opportunities to become more deeply involved. To date, I have invested in eight different franchises as a franchisee and invested in two franchisor businesses.

I have been a franchisor CEO in multiple brands and have been recognised in the Top 30 Franchise Executives in Australia on four occasions, and in 2022 and 2023, I was recognised in the Top 100 Global Influencers in Franchising.

All of this positions me nicely to talk about franchising and what it means to be a franchisee since, through my career, I have personally been involved with and positively impacted over one thousand franchisees.

Coming back to the title, *Invested*, I have invested my whole working life in the franchise sector. I have invested in the ownership of four franchisor brands and eight franchise brands as a franchisee. I know what it means to be invested and what a potential franchisee needs to know before they invest in a franchise. I don't just talk the talk, I walk the talk, and this book refers to my personal experiences with the franchise systems that I have been involved in both as a franchise consultant, an employee, a franchisee, a master franchisee and as a franchisor.

I mentioned earlier the need to be all in, and this is imperative for all franchisees and franchisors; they need to be totally invested in the business and the people working within it. This book will highlight what it means to be invested for the aspiring franchisees, what they should look for in their ideal franchisor and how to evaluate which franchise and franchisor may be right for them or whether they should even go into a franchise or business ownership.

ACKNOWLEDGMENTS

There are many contributors to my life, both personally and professionally. These people have defined who I am as an individual and as a franchise business executive. This is my opportunity to recognise those who have been instrumental in shaping me and my career.

The foundation for my work ethic and knowledge of franchising was formed over 14 years at McDonald's. There is no business with a better franchise system, and that system is made up of outstanding individuals that learn to be outstanding businesspeople, and I thank everyone whom I came into contact with and remain in contact with from McDonald's.

The most successful people I know started at McDonald's, and many of them are still there as franchisees. Although Macquarie Bank has often been referred to as the 'Millionaire Maker', those individuals that stayed at McDonald's and became franchisees are the wealthiest people I know, and that's what this book is about. It shows the strength of a good franchise system and how following a proven model can assist you in becoming successful.

There have been thousands of people that I have worked with since starting my franchise journey back in 1983, and whether they intentionally set about to influence me, everyone I met has influenced me and shaped the person and franchise executive I have become.

There are a few people that I hold close to my heart both as friends, businesspeople, and confidants (George Sleiman, Michael Hansia, John MacPhail and Michael Sleiman, who all worked with me as managers at McDonald's and continue to be my friends). I have been franchise partners with both John Macphail and Michael Hansia. I have admired the tenacity of George Sleiman for what he has achieved in his business. I continue to be inspired by Michael Sleiman for who he is and what he has accomplished in business and life.

My current business partner in Franchise Ready, Peter Elligett, who was my manager and then supervisor at McDonald's, has been working with me and supporting my last two franchisor businesses. We knew that we wanted to work together in our own business, and this became a reality in 2021. Peter is a lot like me, which is good and bad, but he's the guy I can confide in, who has my best interests at heart and will tell me what he thinks, even if I don't want to hear it. Peter has been a successful franchisee, master franchisee and franchisor of two of his own franchise systems, and he brings that knowledge and experience to influence me every day.

The thing that resonates for me with all these gentlemen is their commitment to their families and children, they have strong values, and it is these traits that are needed to be successful in franchising and life.

I am able to write this book because of all the franchisees and franchisors I have worked with, the franchisors that have allowed me to be a franchisee and part of their system and all of the business owners who have trusted me to work with them and be part of their teams. All of you have helped me and contributed to the content of this book and my business success.

I would like to thank the following people for their contribution to the book and sharing their experiences as franchisees with everyone reading this book: Peter Elligett, David Ciantar, Crystal Petzer, Janiene Pollock, Steve and Tanya Palmer, Richard Kentwell and Michael Sleiman.

To the most important people in my life, Lisa, Taylor and Jackson, who inspire me to be the best I can be, and for allowing me to do what I do and share my expertise with so many businesses and business owners, I thank from the bottom of my heart.

In business, you have to be all in, or it just won't work, and that wouldn't be possible without the love, support and cheerleading from the sidelines of those that are closest to you.

CHAPTER 1

WHAT IS FRANCHISING?

It's not a business — it's a way of doing business

"With a franchise, you have someone who cares as much about the business name and image as you do because they own it."
—Jim Evanger

Have you ever heard the term 'disenfranchised' and wondered what it meant? Every time I hear that someone is disenfranchised, I cringe. It is used out of context and relates to a feeling of disappointment that someone may have with their circumstances or a reaction to something they are experiencing.

It's at this time it makes me think about what a franchise is.

To be disenfranchised means to have your legal rights taken away from you. Therefore, to have a franchise means the granting of legal rights. In the case of business, it means the right to use intellectual property that has been developed by an individual through a company. That company can license the rights for an individual or entity to use the system that they have developed.

The concept of franchising is not new. It's been around since the Middle Ages when the government gave licenses to churches and local councils to collect taxes and to landowners to grant rights to individuals to sell their wares and produce.

In 1731, when Benjamin Franklin expanded his print shop business and newspaper production to additional locations, he granted the rights for individuals to use the systems and processes that he had developed and perfected. In so doing, he charged them a fee for these rights.

There are three modern-day franchising heroes: Isaac Singer, Henry Ford and Ray Kroc, who I'd like to mention here for the amazing work they did in pioneering franchising.

Isaac Singer, the inventor of the Singer sewing machine, was a pioneer of modern-day franchising. At the time, most sewing was done by hand. A Singer sewing machine had a significantly greater capacity but one huge limitation — the cost. Singer's response was to offer customers the option to pay for the machine in instalments. This created a huge demand for the product, but Singer now needed a better system of distribution and servicing. His solution was to recruit businesspeople who would pay him an upfront license (franchise) fee for the territorial rights to sell the sewing machines and to provide ongoing service to the customers in the territories where the machines were sold.

Around the same time, Henry Ford was starting to mass-produce motor vehicles. His method of sale was through travelling salesmen, which proved to be unprofitable. So, he licensed two car dealerships, and the Ford Motor Company franchise model was born.

And then there's my personal favourite, Ray Kroc. Ray was not the founder of McDonald's, nor did he come up with the idea of franchising McDonald's. But he certainly perfected it. Ray was a multi-mixer (milkshake maker) salesman who went door-to-door selling multi-mixer machines. The significance of this piece of machinery was that each machine made five milkshakes at once, and the founders of McDonald's — Dick and Maurice, the McDonald brothers — had just put in an order for eight machines. Ray was fascinated and wanted to see why they had made such an order.

After observing their operation, Ray envisaged the McDonald's system being rolled out right across America. Ray couldn't sleep that night with his excitement about the opportunity that the McDonald's business represented.

"When I saw it working that day in 1954, I felt like some latter-day Newton who'd just had an Idaho potato caromed off his skull. That night in my motel room I did a lot of heavy thinking about what I'd seen during the day. Visions of McDonald's restaurants dotting crossroads all over the country paraded through my brain."

—Ray Kroc

Much to Ray's delight, the McDonald's brothers were looking for an agent to sell franchises across the country. With Ray's 30 years in sales, he was in the right place at the right time.

"The two most important requirements for major success are: first, being in the right place at the right time, and second, doing something about it."

—Ray Kroc

Ray cemented a deal to be the McDonald brothers' exclusive agent and started selling franchises. Ray tried to convince the brothers that they should start thinking bigger and continue to expand the business, but the McDonald's brothers were content. They started to put the brakes on Ray and his vision of growing the brand.

Ray ended up buying out the McDonald brothers for $2.7 million after learning that they weren't as motivated as he was in building a restaurant empire.

"The McDonald brothers were simply not on my wavelength at all. I was obsessed with the idea of making McDonald's the biggest and the best. They were content with what they had; they didn't want to be bothered with more risks and more demands."

—Ray Kroc

As you can see, franchising is not a business but a way of leveraging the systems, processes and intellectual property that has been developed and perfected to ensure a smoother transition into a business. Ray Kroc didn't invent it, but he took it more seriously than anyone else.

"We take the hamburger business more seriously than anyone else."

—Ray Kroc

There Are Three Types of Franchise Models

Manufacturing franchises: used by organisations such as Coca-Cola, where a license is issued to another party to make their product.

Coca-Cola's franchising system dates back to 1889, when bottling rights began to be sold to businessmen who were capable of large-scale bottling and thus were able to quickly expand the product into new markets. One of the early 'brand standards' set for the system was an agreement by the bottlers to only sell the product in a standard and unique 'contour' bottle, patented in 1915.

The Coca-Cola Company produces syrup concentrate, then sells it to bottlers around the world, who hold an exclusive territory to bottle and sell the end product. These bottling partners manufacture, package and distribute the finished product to vending partners, who then sell directly to consumers.

Product franchises: used by organisations such as Ford Motor, who issue them to dealers to sell their cars.

Or, as we have seen more recently, movie and television 'franchises' follow a formula and are owned by a group that licenses the rights to produce and screen the productions.

Almost every professional sporting competition in the world includes franchises, where sporting teams are granted the license to operate within a geographical territory. This has been very common in the USA, with baseball franchises being granted in 1876 and every NFL Gridiron team, NHL team, or NBA team operating a franchise issued by their governing body.

Business format franchising: this is the most common form of franchising, where a highly recognised and branded outlet is franchised to a franchisee for them to operate under strict conditions for a fixed term.

Familiar brands that use a business format franchise approach include the majority of the bricks-and-mortar operations, like McDonald's and KFC.

Current-day Franchising

We have experienced some turbulent times with franchising in Australia with parliamentary enquiries into the sector. It seems to see negative press on a weekly basis, but these challenges are not exclusive to Australia, with similar challenges happening globally. The thing is, the stories are headline grabbing and often one sided.

The problem is not franchising per se but a minority of individuals who happen to be in some high-profile franchise organisations. They have done the wrong thing, and this is causing aspersions to be cast on the franchise sector as a whole.

The process of franchising is sound, but it's important to understand that **franchising is not a business — it's a way of doing business**.

People have been doing business since the beginning of time. According to Rudyard Kipling, prostitution was 'the world's oldest profession', when, in fact, there are a number of industries and professions that emerged well before prostitution. These included builders, farmers, musicians, artists, storytellers, clothiers, tailors, hunters, butchers and toolmakers. Why do I mention these professions? Because all of them have been franchised in modern times. Every business has the potential to be scaled, and most businesses have the potential to be licensed or franchised.

It's important to understand a little more about what franchising is, other than its origins or the core principles of it is a license to use the systems and processes of a developed brand.

Marketing Strategy

Franchising is a business strategy for getting and keeping customers. It is a marketing system for creating an image in the minds of current and future customers of how the company's products and services can help them. It is a method for distributing products and services that satisfy customers' needs.

Interdependence

Franchising requires interdependence, where both the franchisee and franchisor have needs to be met.

Interdependence is working within the confines of the requirements of the franchisor for the mutual benefit and consistency of all other franchisees within that system. There is also a dependence on the franchisor to provide leadership, development of the brand, and support for the franchisees.

Dependence is part of any franchise relationship, as the franchisee relies on the franchisor to guide them towards success. But the system alone will not guarantee success. It is up to each franchisee to make the system work for them, and, in turn, they need to work for and within the system.

Independence is ignoring others and any coexistence, wanting to deal with everything alone, and not acknowledging any need for support. Often, franchisors are largely independent operators who want to run their own show. Independent individuals make good franchisors but not necessarily good franchisees.

Franchising is a network of interdependent business relationships that allows a number of people to share:

- A brand identity
- A successful method of doing business
- A proven marketing and distribution system
- A product or service that is differentiated from the competition.

In short, franchising is a strategic alliance between groups of people who have specific relationships and responsibilities, with a common goal to dominate the markets that they operate within.

There are many misconceptions about franchising, but probably the most widely held is that a franchisee is 'buying a franchise'. In reality, the franchisee is investing their assets in a system to utilise the brand name, operating system and ongoing support. Every franchisee in the system is licensed to do this.

If a franchisee was, in fact, 'buying a franchise', they would most likely feel entitled to operate the business the way they would like and would make entrepreneurial decisions about their business that may contradict how the franchisor needs the business to be run.

The key to the success of any franchise system starts with the premise that the franchisor does not sell franchises; they grant the rights for individuals to use the intellectual property of the brand.

CHAPTER 2

FOLLOWING THE RULES

The Legals

The legal landscape is changing — we're becoming a more litigious society, and with that comes stricter guidelines for franchisors. As a franchise consulting business, we help brands scale and grow through franchising, and I would estimate that 80% of the prospective franchisor clients we meet ask if franchising is the right way for them to grow, which is a great question, as long it relates to the right reason for asking that question. I would estimate that 30% ask the question, 'Would it not be cheaper and easier to license their brand to avoid the legalities of franchising?', because they've heard how onerous franchising can be and how expensive it is.

Whenever we meet a prospective client, we complete this very evaluation to determine what are the best ways for those business owners to grow their business, and for some, it may not be franchising.

There are some key questions that we ask to determine if their brand would be classified as a franchise, and they are:

1. If there is a requirement to market the brand based on the IP owner's requirements

2. If an owned trademark or symbol is used
3. If they were granted the rights to trade under the brands' name
4. If there is a charging of an initial and ongoing fee to use the IP
5. If agreements are in place that outline how the IP will be used
6. If the owner of the IP insists on uniforms, recommended pricing, inability to sell other or competing goods and services, mandatory training or suggests the methods for operating the business and how the brand name or logo is used.

If the answer to any of these questions is yes, then these businesses would be deemed a franchise by those that legislate franchise law.

As franchising grows in popularity, the risk increases potentially for unfair contracts and franchisor imbalance of power with their franchisees, and there will be more legislation and minimum requirements of franchisors for disclosure and fairness in contracts.

Australia and the USA lead the world with franchise legislation, where the government monitors and manages the sector. In Australia, there is a strict Franchise Code of Conduct that is legislated and policed by the ACCC. In countries where there are no franchise laws, the franchising bodies and associations are pushing for change because they know the benefit to all parties and where it is not legislated many associations make it a condition of membership to their franchise associations to meet certain minimum disclosure requirements in addition to the contract law of their country.

It's really just a matter of time before all countries embrace the rigour of disclosure and the lead that Australia and the USA have adopted. Both countries have a consistent regulation for the franchising sector that contributes to the success of the sector in these countries. In countries where it is not legislated, then it is a best practice by those franchisors that follow the lead of those countries already regulated.

The reality is that franchising and the laws that govern it are good for franchisors and obviously good for the franchisees that the legislation was created for.

Franchising is a growing sector and represents up to 15% of total businesses operating throughout the world, and with greater numbers of individuals using franchising as the way for them to enter business ownership, many governments have legislated laws to protect franchisees. In so doing, they are effectively protecting franchisors by giving protection and credibility to franchising as a way of doing business.

Where there is no or little regulation, it is possible for franchisors to take advantage of franchisees and in many countries, this has forced governments to legislate.

The Two Key Legal Documents

Are you ready for some late-night reading? Don't be concerned by the size of the legal documents you receive or the legal jargon contained within. Most franchise documents range in length between 40–120 pages which may seem daunting, and in some cases, the legalise can be a little painful, but it's there for a reason, and your franchisor and your legal advisor will be able to explain everything that is contained within those documents. Most franchise documents are written in plain language, and most potential franchisees will read and understand 90% of what is contained within the documents.

It's my recommendation to get your hands on the proforma version of the franchise documents early in your discovery process. Most franchisors will want to adequately qualify you before they give you access to their proforma documents, but early receipt of these can speed up the process when you decide to proceed or can assist you in evaluating the opportunity without incurring too much time or money on an opportunity that may not be right for you.

It is advisable for you to read the franchise documents and get comfortable with the clauses contained within them, compile a list of questions and concerns that you can discuss with the franchisor and with your legal counsel. I strongly recommend that you seek independent legal advice, and that advice should be with a commercial franchising lawyer that understands franchise law. Otherwise, you may not get the right advice, or the legal review may be time consuming and costly. In Australia, franchisors must advise you to obtain professional legal, financial and accounting advice, and there are certificates that need to be signed by your advisors. However, you can choose not to obtain that professional advice and you will then need to sign those certificates of advice acknowledging that the franchisor informed you to obtain the advice and you have chosen not to.

If you want to attempt negotiation of even minor points in your franchise documents, you should have a lawyer negotiate for you. Lawyers are trained to handle legal matters and have more credibility than you do alone. Furthermore, negotiations can quickly become more complicated than your experience can handle, so it's to your advantage to have a legal expert handling them for you.

I cannot emphasise enough that you should get a commercial franchising lawyer to assist you with the review of the franchise documents to protect you and ensure that you understand exactly what you are getting into. Don't get your family lawyer to advise you, franchising is a specialised field, and although it may appear easier going with someone you know or is cheaper, it may actually cost you more. Franchise lawyers are familiar with the franchise laws and know what to look for when reviewing franchise documents on your behalf.

My recommendation is for you to read the franchise documents and highlight the areas of concern or areas that you don't understand and have your legal counsel focus on those, together with a general review of the key terms, commercials and anomalies that they have experienced drafting franchise documents and reviewing other franchise documents. I would estimate that you should budget between $2,000–$3,000 for this legal support.

The Franchise Agreement

A franchise agreement is a binding contract enforceable by law. Franchising is often referred to as a marriage between two parties; there's the courtship, the honeymoon and then the reality of the relationship comes into play and just like some marriages, franchise relationships can break down. The franchise agreement sets out the rules of engagement and unlike a contract of marriage, it may be harder to exit a franchise, so you need to understand your obligations.

The franchise agreement sets out your obligations; it's the rule book for the business and what the franchisee needs to adhere to.

What's in a franchise agreement?

Here are the main provisions covered in most franchise contracts. It's important to know what to expect before looking at contracts so that you can make an informed decision about whether to accept a franchisor's terms. Franchise contracts are legally binding, so be sure that you can abide by the terms before signing.

Franchise territory and boundaries

Each franchise location covers a certain area, which is spelt out by the franchise contract. These territories may be exclusive or non-exclusive, and it's important that you understand the consequences of both and what the potential may be for your territory if the franchisor decides to open other franchises near yours.

Often, exclusive territories are exclusive for the purposes of marketing, meaning you will have the exclusive rights to market the business within your territory and no other franchisee can encroach on your territory. However, it does not mean that a customer cannot use an adjacent franchisees' products or services. At the end of the day, the customer chooses who they want to buy from.

Typically, other franchisees cannot set up their locations within a certain distance of your territory, and this is spelt out in the agreement or through a territory map with boundaries.

Ask your prospective franchisor how they determine a territory and boundaries. Many franchisors use sophisticated territory mapping to scientifically define boundaries, and most will share this data with you and explain the rationale for the territory boundaries and what constitutes a potential territory.

Length of the franchise agreement

The typical duration of a franchise agreement is usually 5 or 10 years but can be as long as 20 years, in the case of McDonald's. Often the term of the franchise agreement is tied to the lease term for a bricks-

and-mortar business. For instance, in shopping centres, landlords like to refurbish their centres every five years, so a common lease term inside a shopping centre typically marries up to that.

It may be prudent to negotiate a longer term as this will enable you to get a better return on your investment. In franchising, the average return on capital investment is around three years for bricks-and-mortar businesses, so you want to leave yourself enough time to generate profit over and above receiving your initial investment back.

This part of the contract will also spell out the conditions under which the franchise can be sold to someone else, which can be stringent to make sure that any future franchisee is qualified to be an owner. Sometimes, there will be a right of first refusal clause that allows the franchisor to buy back the franchise rather than have it sold to someone else.

Be mindful of any obligations to make minimum payments for the term of the agreement in the event that you decide to cease the franchise. A longer franchise term potentially locks you into ongoing payments if you are unable to sell your franchise to another party. This happened to me with one of my franchise investments, and I was locked into paying $2,000 a month for a business I was not even working in. There is the potential to negotiate a buy-out clause in the event that you do leave the franchise system, and some franchisors will include this in their agreements but you may like to ask for this provision to be inserted. My recommendation would be to offer 25% of the fees for the remaining term or until the business is resold, whichever comes first.

Franchise costs and fees

There is a schedule of costs in the franchise agreement and a more detailed summary of all expenses you may incur in the franchise disclosure document. Besides the initial franchise fee, this part of the contract covers the costs involved in owning a franchise, including monthly royalties, advertising and marketing requirements, whether there is a co-operative marketing fund and/or requirements for you to conduct localised marketing and what is the percentage of revenue or fixed dollar amount for this marketing. It will outline the legal costs to issue the franchise documents to you, which is in addition to your own legal counsel to review these documents. There are some other costs to enter the franchise system, and these are stipulated in the franchise agreement and are typically not negotiable. They are the hard costs of entering the franchise system, while the variable costs are outlined in the franchise disclosure document.

Many franchise contracts also include stipulations on how much cash franchisees must have available before purchasing the unit; this is called the debt-to-equity ratio. Franchisors will include this to ensure that a franchisee has enough working capital to fund the business and that their borrowings don't impede on the cash flow and profitability of the business. A good rule of thumb is to only borrow up to 50% of the investment cost.

The fees in the agreement that you sign remain the same for the duration of your franchise term, but they may change with the sale of the franchise or at the expiration of the term of the franchise agreement. If the franchisor sells the business, the terms that you signed remain for the duration of your franchise agreement unless agreed to change by both parties.

Trademarks and patents

The franchisor owns the trademark, various patents, logos and the signage associated with the franchise. Their operations manuals and standard operating procedures are copyrighted, so they may not be used outside of the franchise. This part of the contract outlines the specific ways a franchisee is permitted to use those entities, as well as the ways they are not permitted to use them.

Rules for operating

Each franchise has specific rules for the way franchisees must run their units. These can include hours of operation, specific items or services sold, and pay rates for employees, among many other things. Managerial structure, software programs used, and the way a franchise location must be laid out are other items that may fall under rules for operating.

The franchise agreement will reference the operations manual, which allows the franchisor to change operational standards as the business develops for the overall benefit of the franchise system. The franchisor cannot make wholesale changes to the operating methods or standards without agreement by the franchise network, but it reserves its right to make changes and improvements to the business through changes made in the operations manual.

Franchise renewal rights and termination policies

Specifics about how a franchise can be renewed and under what conditions it can be terminated are included in this section. If a situation arises where the franchisor and franchisee are in conflict, there may be an arbitration clause that requires a process, which may include mediation and/or conciliation prior to escalation to legal action through the courts. It is at these hearings an arbitrator reviews the case, makes a recommendation to both parties and attempts to assist with the brokering of an outcome.

The franchise agreement will indicate under what circumstances a renewal term may be granted. Normally, a franchisee has the rights to renew subject to them not being in breach and the franchisor believing that the franchise unit is a viable business. Many franchise agreements have a provision for a renewal fee to grant and additional franchise term to the sitting franchisee.

Each party has obligations regarding termination, and the franchisees' obligations are spelt out in the franchise agreement, while the franchisors' obligations relating to termination are determined by contract law and disclosure requirements legislated in those countries that have disclosure requirements.

It's important to know that there needs to be fairness in contracts and that the franchisor must follow a process for terminating a franchise agreement. This includes the issuing of a breach notice and a period of time for the franchisee in which to remedy the breach.

Training and support provided by the franchisor

It is standard for franchisors to train new franchisees and to give them ongoing support. Franchises are built around uniform business practices, and training will help new franchisees understand what is expected of them and learn the practices that have given the franchise company success. Ongoing support can take the form of continuing training for franchisees, managers and team members. All franchisors are required to make available an operations manual and training program to ensure the franchisee understands how to use the system. Many franchisors are using online learning management systems to house all the operational and training resources making them available in the cloud with standard operating procedures (SOPs), videos, testing and auditing functions making them easy to access by being stored in the cloud.

Franchisors hold regular franchise meetings and training sessions for their franchisees, and these are usually included in the initial training fee or franchise fee and as part of the ongoing franchise royalty fee. From time to time, the franchisor may bring in external trainers and run dedicated training events. These may be at the franchisees' cost, but they will be outlined in the franchise agreement. Remedial or additional training may be provided or deemed necessary for a franchisee that is underperforming, and this will be charged to the franchisee if the franchisor is required to administer this remedial training.

Franchisors will provide ongoing support to their franchisees through communications platforms online, in-person meetings, online meetings, franchise conferences and field visits by the field support personnel. The amount of this support is based on the needs of the franchisee and the complexity of the business operation. Some businesses will only receive a field visit annually whilst others may see the representative every month. Each of these visits will be documented so the franchisee has a record of what their current performance is and what areas may need attention. These audits ensure consistency across the network and form the basis of determining the operational compliance of the franchisee and suitability to continue trading and offering of a franchise renewal when required. It is in the franchisor's interest to support their franchisees to be the best that they can be and that all franchisees have access to the franchisor support team any day during office hours.

Can you negotiate the terms of a franchise contract?

The vast majority of franchisors are not open to negotiating their franchise contracts. It is advisable to have a lawyer with franchise experience look at any potential franchise contract and give you an honest assessment about which parts of the contract may or may not be advantageous for you as the franchisee.

It is important to note, however, that the franchisor's main goal in the contract is to protect the value and integrity of the franchise as a whole, as well as it should be. If the entire franchise fails, none of the franchisees will have anything left. For this reason, most franchisors don't negotiate their franchise contracts, and it may even be unrealistic to expect franchisors to go out of their way to accommodate franchisees.

Some emerging franchisors may be more negotiable because the questions may not have been posed to them previously, and often, when a franchise agreement is drafted by the franchisor's lawyer, it is done to protect the franchise system and can be onerous. I have always held the view that if the question the franchisee or their lawyer is asking makes sense, then we should make the change.

If you find clauses in the contract that are non-negotiable for you, you can ask questions of your potential franchisor to find out why those clauses were included and whether the franchisor would consider taking them out of the contract, but chances are the franchisor will not negotiate on anything of any importance. If you feel the contract is unfavourable and would prevent you from getting a good return on your investment, your best bet is probably to pursue a different franchise with more favourable terms.

Why negotiable contracts may not be a good thing for franchisees?

There are good reasons why franchisors don't typically negotiate contracts. Most franchises have been in existence for years and have developed successful business models. They usually know what works far better than their franchisees do, and so, they insist on setting up the contract in a way that they know will work out well for both them and the franchisees.

In addition, franchisors have other franchisees that they have worked with before the current location. If they negotiate with you, how will their existing franchisees react? Negotiating might open up a door for existing franchisees to demand the same deal you got or to become unsatisfied with their own contracts. Franchisors would naturally want to avoid this, which explains the policy of not negotiating contracts.

It is actually a sign of strength on the franchisor's part not to negotiate with potential franchisees. It shows confidence in the success of their previous contracts and in their system of franchising. You should ask if negotiation is possible, but if the franchisor seems willing to negotiate any major points of the contract, it could very well be a red flag that there is some flaw in their business model. You may want to proceed with caution.

Negotiations are uncommon for franchise contracts but sometimes do happen for smaller items, and some early-stage franchisors may be more negotiable on the commercial terms rather than the legal provisions as they want to get their first few franchisees signed up. They typically won't negotiate on the ongoing royalties or marketing fund expenses as they need to be consistent across the group, but there may be some wiggle room on the initial franchise fees and some of the ancillary costs. However, once the brand has established value in the franchise, the franchisor will not negotiate the commercial aspects.

Small negotiations you may be able to make

There are some minor negotiations that may be possible with some franchise contracts. In these small areas, you may be able to get more favourable terms, but it won't really affect the main operations of the franchise. Newer, less established franchises are usually more likely to be willing to negotiate than well-established ones.

Instalment terms for your franchise fee (vendor finance)

If the emerging franchisor won't discount the initial franchise fee, it may be worth asking them to vendor finance the cost on agreed terms or through a higher ongoing franchise royalty until the amount of the initial franchise fee is paid. If a franchisor agrees to this, they may request an interest component on the amount being vendor financed, and they will set up a vendor loan agreement to reflect this.

The franchise disclosure document (FDD)

The FDD helps potential franchisees make an informed decision about the franchise they are considering entering into. Disclosure documents are laid out in much the same format and often reflect the franchise law of the jurisdiction that they are issued. In Australia, this is detailed in the Franchise Code of Conduct, administered by the ACCC. There is a requirement for certain information to be included in the disclosure document, even if that information may be discouraging for the franchisee reading it.

The disclosure document must provide current information about the franchisor and what the franchisee needs to know to operate the business. The disclosure document needs to be updated once per year. This disclosure document needs to be updated within four months of the end of the financial year and should reflect the changes in the franchisor's business in the previous 12 months. Unless a franchisee requests an updated version of the disclosure document, the franchisor does not have to update it unless they entered into more than one new franchise agreement or they don't intend to grant any further franchise agreements in that new year.

If significant changes in the franchisor's business happen, the franchisor cannot delay informing the existing franchisees or potential franchisees about the changes, meaning they cannot wait until the new year to communicate such major changes or issues that may affect the business.

Red Flags When Reviewing Franchise Contracts

Having a lawyer go over your franchise contract should catch most of these issues, but in the overall franchise acquisition process, there are some situations that should give you pause. Here are some red flags that should cause you to proceed with caution.

Being Rushed into Signing

The research process should take as long as you need to feel comfortable. Generally, the 'courtship' period, when you are getting to know the franchisor and the opportunity, can take as little as a month and as long as a year, depending on the cost and complexity of the business and the legislative requirements. Do your due diligence and answer all the questions that you and your advisors have and use the checklists of questions provided in this book to ensure you go into the franchise with full disclosure and understanding of what both parties' obligations are and will be.

In some countries like Australia, it is legislated that a franchisor cannot force a franchisee into signing an agreement without them following the law that has been set down, which includes the professional advisor requirements and the mandatory time frame for consideration of the opportunity. In Australia, once a franchisee decides they would like to move forward with an opportunity, they request formal franchise legal documents to be drafted (this normally takes one–two weeks to draft). Once the franchisee has the agreements, they seek the independent advice of a lawyer, accountant and financial advisor and they need to consider these documents for a minimum of 14 days before they can sign the agreements. After they sign the agreements, they have a further 14-day cooling-off period during which they can rescind the contract. Some franchisors may put their own timelines on this process, but they cannot negotiate the legal requirements. A good rule of thumb is that if you feel pressured, this may not be the right opportunity.

You need to be fair with the franchisor as they are investing significantly in you, so if the opportunity is not right, let them know as soon as possible.

Discounting Prices

Quality franchises know the value of their franchise opportunity, what their competitors are offering and where they are positioned against them, so discount prices may indicate a lack of quality. Carefully investigate the reason for the discount. If it's to make franchisees feel as though they are getting a bargain, that's one thing, but if it's due to a lack of interest in the franchise opportunity, then you will want to research its potential very carefully before committing.

Withholding Documents

I mentioned earlier that if you can obtain the proforma franchise agreement and disclosure document, this can speed up the process and assist you in determining if this may be the right franchise for you without wasting time and money on a system that may not be right for you.

The FDD includes contact information for the executive team as well as detailed information about the franchise's financials and any legal cases that may have been filed against it. Franchisors may hold back giving you access to these documents until they know that you are bona fide and have met their selection criteria. Many franchisors will have an established recruitment process that works for them, and you need to respect this. It is unlikely, but some franchisors may not make these documents available to you as they may not be conducive to you looking at them favourably. If a franchisor has nothing to hide, they will make these proforma documents available to you when the time is right, just be sure to ask them when that will be and why you would like the information (to show you are serious and to potentially speed up the process).

Lists of Franchisees to Call

Most disclosure documents will include a list of both present and past franchisees and their contact details. The latter may be a reason why the franchisor is unwilling to provide you with the disclosure document as this contains these details. These exited franchisees are not in themselves a red flag, but if the franchisor discourages you from talking to franchisees or specifies who you should talk to, that could be a red flag. Franchisors shouldn't have anything to hide and should be open to your talking to anyone you wish within the business.

I am a strong believer that not everyone is right for business, for franchising and for particular franchises, so people leaving a franchise system or even potentially being bitter is just part of life and business. Ultimately, every franchise system has some disgruntled franchisees.

Asking the right questions of them and other franchisees will give you an accurate read on the franchisor and the franchise system.

The Financials

In order for you to make an informed decision about the franchise opportunity, you need to know the commercials and the detail of the business model, which is how they make money and what the costs to make the revenue are and ultimately, what is left over as profit. I cover this in quite some detail in chapter 7 and chapter 9.

If the franchisor is an early-stage/emerging franchisor, their financials may not be a robust as an established franchisor, but all franchisors should be able to give you the accurate costs of operating and revenue for their existing company-operated locations. Franchisors cannot represent what you may be able to achieve, you have to form this view through your own research, but having the franchisor provide company unit financials or having franchisees provide you with data will be beneficial in evaluating the opportunity.

Franchisors do not need to share their entire P&L with you but should make available the key performance indicators (KPIs) to you for your evaluation. These include revenue across existing locations, cost of goods (COGs) as a percentage, labour costs as a percentage, including franchisee/manager's hours worked and paid, and copies of sample rosters from different revenue thresholds and rental for leased sites so you can see the occupancy cost, these are the key numbers that you need to know.

COGS and labour costs represent 50–70% of revenue, and this can make or break a business. Ask to see actual labour reports and rosters and obtain costings of the menu items and a quality cost report that shows the projected COGs and compare this to the actual COGs to see if a business has good controls. Then, ask the franchisor how they assist their franchisees in improving sales and profitability because the best franchisors focus on this, not just on top-line revenue and collecting franchise royalties.

Some early-stage franchisors' total P&Ls may not be attractive as they have been heavily investing in growing the brand, so you need to normalise any numbers that are shared with you.

In more mature businesses, the franchisor has more data and will make available to you a range of data, including the lower, middle and upper quartile of franchise performances, so you can see how each category of franchisee performs. This allows you to see the best and worst and ask questions around these performances by franchisee.

Early-stage franchisors do not have to share the franchisor entity operating P&L until their third year of operation. Until then, they are only required to include an audit report from an independent auditor about their ability to meet their financial obligations. All established franchisors that have been trading for more than two years will include the franchisor financials in the FDD so you can see how the business is performing for them.

CHAPTER 3

BUYING YOURSELF A JOB

Business Ownership versus Self-employment

"Every business owner is self-employed, but not every self-employed person is a business owner."
—Doug Downer

Around 16% of the world's eligible working population get into business ownership, and they do this for several reasons: it may be to be their own boss, to take control of their life and future, to be proud to be a business owner and, hopefully, to be more financially independent and successful than they would be if remaining in paid employment. It is estimated that business owners generate an income that is 30% higher than had they stayed in employment.

There is a distinction between (1) self-employment and business ownership and (2) entrepreneurship and franchising, and it is important to understand the differences.

Self-Employment and Business Ownership

Both options are good, but there are unique differences that the individual needs to be aware of. Quite simply, the difference is encapsulated in the quote, 'Every business owner is self-employed, but not every self-employed person is a business owner'.

Every person that goes into business has made a conscious decision to do something for themselves and to create an income stream to sustain their lifestyle. Self-employment relies heavily on the individual to do the work, generate the revenue and control the costs. If the individual takes time off, typically, the revenue stops, and there is no continuity.

The difference with the business owner is the individual is involved in many aspects of the business, but there is a system and resources to ensure the revenue continues if the owner is not there.

Simply put, if you can't take 10–12 weeks away from your business, you may be classified as self-employed.

There are excellent franchise opportunities for both self-employment and business ownership. Nevertheless, self-employed businesses are slightly harder to sell because they rely on the owner, and there is no guarantee of continuity of revenue, whereas the business is less dependent on the business owner because they have systems and resources to ensure the revenue continues in their absence, and this results in an easier sale and a higher sale multiple when you choose to sell.

The business owner relies on people and needs to lead and manage these people to get results. The self-employed may prefer to work on their own or in a small team without the worry of leading and managing others. It is this evaluation a prospective franchisee needs to make when evaluating which franchise may be right for them.

Having said all of that, the premise of franchising is that the business will work better if the owner is actively involved in the day-to-day operations, so this is required with both options.

Entrepreneurship and Franchising

In my opinion, not all business owners or franchisees are entrepreneurs. There's a distinction between an entrepreneur and a franchise owner that needs to be defined. The description of each is not 100% accurate but indicative when we profile the two types of business owners.

1. Characteristics of a Franchisee

- Straight-A student
- Long tenure with job
- Corporate job
- Drives a family car
- Few speeding/traffic fines
- Married
- Looking for security.

2. Characteristics of an Entrepreneur

- B or C-student
- Moved from job to job
- Owned businesses
- Drives a sports car
- Lots of speeding/traffic fines
- Divorced
- 'Never saw a rule they didn't want to break'.

This is not to say that franchisees can't become entrepreneurs. The fact that they have left the safety of paid employment for self-employment shows that they have an entrepreneurial spirit. Franchising just makes it safer, and many franchisees will remain franchisees of single or multiple franchise units. For those that scale their business enterprises and take on multiple units, they have to have a different skill set and be more entrepreneurial.

I have seen a lot of franchisees 'cut their teeth' on franchising and then go on to create their own business. Traditionally, franchisees are not entrepreneurs in the true sense of the word, but franchising helps them to be entrepreneurial.

In chapter five, I delve into the three archetypal business owner types: the Craftsman, the Freedom Fighter and the Mountain Climber. All three have greater aspirations than merely being an employee, but all have a unique approach to what is right for them as business owners.

The Great Resignation

There's been a lot of talk about the Great Resignation. Originating in the USA, it was coined by Professor Anthony Klotz to signify the change in workplace behaviours of employees in the wake of the pandemic. Continued talk about this has influenced other parts of the world for many of the same reasons experienced in the USA. Discussion on this topic has resulted in people reflecting on what it means to them, and this has driven and perpetuated this notion of the Great Resignation and gotten people to consider a change in their own situation.

The pandemic and change in working conditions with stand downs, lay-offs, reduced hours and terminations caused periods of uncertainty for employees, but many were protected by government support, particularly lower-paid employees. In most countries, government reaction to employee payments had mixed success but, for the most part, protected employees that were unable to work. In Australia, we had a few different support provisions at each stage of the pandemic and subsequent shutdowns of industry. In retail and hospitality (which represent 60% of franchised business opportunities), we had the unique situation where those employees were unable to attend their workplace but were guaranteed a minimum payment, often significantly higher than what they were receiving for the hours they actually worked before the pandemic. So, we had a significant number of people at home being paid to do nothing. This created a shift in people's mindset around entitlement and a reconsideration of whether they actually wanted to return to work. This coupled with over 600,000 temporary visa holders leaving our shores created a huge shortfall in talent, as many of these visa holders were employed in retail and hospitality. This created a huge shortfall in retail and hospitality businesses and meant many businesses traded fewer hours or owners and family members ended up working more.

For many workers, their employment was made more flexible and those that were not required to be in a fixed location were given the opportunity to work from home and given flexibility, including reduced hours, subsidies from the government, making up the difference in the reduction in hours and with all of this more leisure time at home without a significant impact on lifestyle. People were working less, travelling less and being paid comparably the same, and this caused people to evaluate the way they wanted to work moving forward.

Once the marketplace started to get back to normal with travel restrictions, social distancing and other restrictions put in place throughout the pandemic were lifted, people had gotten used to their new work status. For many, it provided them time to re-evaluate what they really wanted from work and life and the role that work played in their lives.

The workplace has changed, and many businesses have been forced to change with it by offering more flexibility and acknowledging that people have enjoyed working less and working on their terms, and this has created a shift in the balance of power from employers to employees. Those employers that have not adapted have encountered employees leaving their employ either for better work–life balance or for more salary because the market for talent has become more competitive.

In Australia, we haven't so much seen the Great Resignation; it's more like the Great Reshuffle. The working landscape has changed, the war for talent is back, and employees hold the dominant position, while employers have to change to keep people.

In periods of low changing employment, franchising tends to do well because when people can't find work or want to do something different, they look for opportunities in other places, and that's where business ownership, self-employment and franchising tend to boom. In some cases, people end up 'buying themselves a job'. This is not a bad thing; it drives the economy, which creates more jobs, and it enables the business owners to work on their terms and in so doing, it mirrors what is happening with the Great Resignation.

Everybody has different expectations of what their working life will look like and what buying into a franchise business means to them. I have spoken with franchisors that both like and dislike the concept of people buying themselves a job through franchising. Some franchisors want a franchisee with more of an ownership mindset than someone simply changing from paid employment to self-employment business ownership. The reality is that when a person invests in a franchise, they have to take on an ownership mindset and approach to the business like an owner otherwise the business will not perform at its optimum. The concern that franchisors have is if someone is satisfied with just taking a wage, they may not optimise the opportunity and have the business reach its potential, which, in turn, drives the franchisors' revenue through royalty payments.

Whilst the concept of buying yourself a job is a sound one, there is a cost to the franchisee to do this, and it is not sufficient to just get paid a wage as the franchisee has to invest capital in establishing the franchise business. This debt or investment needs to be paid back to the business owner on fair commercial terms. Given that most leases and franchise agreements are for five years the franchisee needs to be getting at least 20% more than their wage just to cover the cost of getting into the business, let alone building equity in the business for all their hard work.

In summary, it's OK to buy yourself a job, but you need to make sure that the business has the potential to generate a fair return on your capital and time. This is just as important for the franchisor as they want successful franchisees in their network because that makes it easier to find other franchisees.

Now assuming that you do decide to go into business ownership, it's important to know the difference between paid employment and business ownership, and it comes down to ownership mindset and ownership thinking.

Ownership Thinking

There is a significant difference between an employee mindset and an ownership mindset, and there is nothing wrong with either. It's a personal choice, and quite frankly, as a business owner, we need employees, as they are the lifeblood of our business. The best business has employees who help the owner achieve their goals by taking on responsibilities that the owner can't, or doesn't want to, do.

Business owners make things happen, they take risks and they think long term, hence the need to be strategic, while the employee waits for direction and to be told what to do. If you're a business owner, your business typically won't yield a consistent level of income for a few years potentially. But when it does, it will be significantly higher than the income of the majority of employees (with the exception of highly paid senior executives in blue chip firms). In fact, more than 65% of millionaires are business owners.

Employees typically think short term, many are risk adverse and yearn for security. They wait to be paid, whereas the business owners get paid when they want.

The goal of any business owner should be to encourage an ownership mindset among their employees so that the employees work together with the business owner to achieve goals more quickly.

An ownership mindset is where an individual or team takes accountability for the quality and success of both the outputs and outcomes of their work. Both of these are important, as ownership doesn't mean perfection. It means knowing why you are doing the work (the outcome) and making sure that what you produce (the output) is at the required standard. It means understanding, learning, and challenging rather than following instructions.

The franchisee that takes on a franchise needs to shift their mindset from anything they have done previously (unless, of course, they have been a franchisee before) because they will understand the difference between employment and business ownership to some degree. If you own an independent business, you determine what you do and when; if you're an employee, your employer has expectations that you need to meet; but if you take on a franchise, you're somewhere in between. That's because you have to follow rules and you don't typically get to set them; simultaneously, you're running a business which means the buck stops with you, but you don't have that support system or team of resources that you may have had access to when you were in paid employment. Furthermore, you do have some freedom to come and go as you please, but you also have the financial implications of those decisions and the requirements of the franchisor and landlords to be open at certain times.

Becoming a franchisee is a unique situation, and you need to be prepared for it. Asking other franchisees will give you the best insight into how this may change your perception of business ownership and the reality of being a franchise business owner. Either way, you have to change your mindset and accept total responsibility for your circumstances. Often, franchisees that still have that employee mindset may point the finger at the franchisor when things don't go to plan. Here's the thing that you need to know: if a franchisor has invested in becoming a franchised business, they have invested a lot and they have demonstrated a proof of concept. If, for whatever reason, it doesn't work, this really falls back on the franchisee, their due diligence and the way they operate the franchise system.

If you become a franchisee, you must take ownership of the performance and outcomes of your business. The franchisor has given you the tools, so you must put them to work, and the success of your franchise business is 100% on you. If you approach franchising with this mindset, then you have a greater chance of success.

This might sound strange, but I had a very successful franchisee in one of the systems I joined, and he said to me, 'I understand the success of the business is entirely on me, anything I get from the franchisor after I joined was a bonus'. This is a refreshing way to look at it, after all, the franchisor has worked hard to establish a successful business model and provide franchisees with the opportunity to leverage their brand and IP, but the best franchisors will also work tirelessly to help franchisees be successful. If franchisees aren't successful, then franchisors can't be successful, so whilst the business success is 100% on you as the franchisee, the best franchisor is invested in your success and will do whatever it can to support your success.

All too often, I have seen people come out of paid employment and move into franchising but not take ownership for the performance of their business, often blaming the franchisor. It is all about mindset and accountability: if you have done your research and due diligence on the franchisor and the business that you have bought into, the success of the franchise business is on you, you have to take on an owner mindset and accept you are the determining factor in your businesse's success or failure.

CHAPTER 4

THE FOUR-LETTER F-WORD

Have you got the guts?

"I never get the accountants in before I start up a business. It's done on gut feeling."
—Richard Branson

I remember attending a sales training session where the facilitator posed the question, 'Do we, as human beings, desire pleasure or the avoidance of pain?' Having not heard that before, I automatically thought, 'I want pleasure', but as he went on to explain, if we had to prioritise the two choices, many of us want to avoid pain, and if we do so, we are moving towards pleasure.

What often holds us back in life is the F-word — fear.

Many of us fear the pain that comes with failure, and failure comes from not meeting our own expectations or those that others have of us. Business ownership is all about that, and we decide if we want to continue doing what we are currently doing or do something different to get a different result. Ultimately, it's about moving away from the pain of our current situation and moving closer to something that will give us more pleasure. Sounds easy, but the reality is that going into business is anything but easy. It is made easier by going into a franchise business because much of the development (hard) work has been done before and the system works.

Some considering business ownership dislike what they are currently doing, and it is causing them 'pain' of some kind, and they want that to change it, while other people may be comfortable and 'pain' free in their current role.

If we are comfortable in our everyday life and we are not experiencing pain, why change? Why take risks? Usually, because we want more, whatever that more may be. For those that consider business ownership, there can be several motivating factors, we may be unhappy in our current role, we may want the freedom to do what we want when we want, we may want the opportunity to improve our position, be that financial or hierarchical, we may have always had a yearning for being our own boss. If you're reading this book, you've probably had those thoughts, but something is holding you back, and for a lot of us, it's fear. As human beings, we don't like change, we don't like risk and we don't like the pain associated with failure.

Now you're probably thinking, 'That's right, Doug, I've worked hard to get what I've got, and I don't want to risk it'. But here's the thing: you're reading this book, which means you want to do it, but you just need to some help to minimise the risk and help you make a good decision.

That's what this book is all about. I love franchising, I love business and I love being a business owner, but every time I have started a new business, I was paralysed with fear because none of us like to lose what we've worked so hard to build. But as long as you do your research and follow the principles outlined in this book, you have a significantly better chance of success.

In this chapter, I am going to discuss two aspects of 'guts'. As I see it, guts come into play in many ways as a business owner. Traditionally, when people refer to 'guts' in business, they refer to the courage to make decisions. I want to expand that and consider one other relevant reference to guts.

"All our dreams can come true if we have the courage to pursue them."
—Walt Disney

There are three inspirational stories of courage and persistence that I resonate with.

I love the story of Colonel Harland Sanders being rejected by 1,009 restaurants before one took on his recipe.

Walt Disney was turned down by 302 banks before getting the finance to fund Disneyland and was fired from the *Kansas City Star* because the editor thought he 'lacked imagination and had no good ideas'.

Steve Jobs was sacked from Apple, the company he founded, but he came back and turned the business around.

The Two Guts You Need to Use in Business

Guts in Business

Many business owners can relate to this: the feelings when they questioned why they ever got into business. They contemplate how to get out. They've probably had that sick feeling in the pit of their stomach to the point of actually being sick, worrying about the state of their business and the impact it had on the people around them and those that they love. I know I have!

It was so much safer and, at times more, enjoyable to be an employee with a guaranteed salary, holiday and sick leave, bonuses, and incentives. Being able to clock off at the end of the day and not have to worry about work until the next day because you were only responsible to yourself and the role you fulfilled. As a business owner, you're responsible for everyone and everything. There's no IT or marketing department to call on, no financial controller and surplus funds in the bank account to meet payroll obligations or pay your suppliers when they're due.

You are no longer just responsible for your income. There's your family's welfare, your assets and everything that you've worked so hard for. There are the employees who are part of your team, who you think of as your extended family. As a business owner, you have their livelihood and that of their families in your hands.

Why would anyone go into business? It takes guts, and it's all about risk. I believe there are 'risk-seekers' and 'risk-tolerators'. All business owners are risk-takers, and while you must be, the key is the calculated risk.

It might sound a little irresponsible to term a group of business owners as risk-seekers because no one should actively seek risk. But there is an inevitability associated with business ownership that involves risk, and some business owners are more comfortable with risk.

Risk-seekers derive excitement from uncertainty. Have you ever driven your car around on empty when you could have just as easily filled up earlier? Do you ever schedule that extra meeting, when in reality, there is no possible way you can fit it in? Heaven forbids you might have even run late for a flight or missed one completely, or dare I say it, been late for a meeting.

There's a strong chance that if you're a risk-seeker, you like the adrenaline rush. You've probably driven too fast, bungee jumped, skydived, been around wild animals, or partaken in other adrenaline-junkie-type activity.

Risk-seekers are impatient and like doing multiple things because we get a bit bored with too much detail, and we make decisions quickly. I'm only up to chapter 5, and I'm already thinking about when I can publish this book and what the title and theme of my next book should be.

Risk-tolerators do not necessarily see risk as risk. They pursue their goals by understanding, accepting, managing the inherent risks of the decisions that they make.

I have had partners in seven of my businesses. I should probably start off by sharing with you that I am a risk-seeker, but I would only classify myself as mid-level and by no means extreme. I have a few of those kinds of business owners I coach and consult with; more about them a little later.

This may not be indicative of every business situation, but four of my business partners have been risk-tolerators, and coincidentally, each of these has been excellent businesses that have been very financially rewarding. My other three business partners were probably more like me, and while the partnership was fun, it was nowhere near as profitable as it could have been.

The risk-tolerant business owner spends more time analysing, understanding, and assessing the risks at hand, learning how best to mitigate them. These risk-tolerant individuals confront fear not with the risk-seeker's optimism, but with thoughtful analysis, management, and self-awareness techniques.

You can't decide which one you want to be. I think it is inherent in your DNA, but what we need to do, whichever risk profile you have in business, is learn and borrow from each type of person and take on the characteristics of each profile.

Where Do Guts Come From?

The willingness to take risks is a combination of factors. I use DISC behavioural profiling quite a bit in my business, and there are some common traits and profiles associated with risk-seeking and risk-tolerant profiles. The factors that influence your preference are a result of your life and business experiences, which include the results you've encountered, when you've taken risks previously, and the support network you have around you.

External factors aside, some people are just more risk-hungry than others. While you cannot choose what degree of guts you're born with, it can help to know if you're naturally fearless, genetically risk-averse, or somewhere in between.

As an entrepreneur and business owner, you will likely have to deal with some failure. It may be small, like a bad product launch or the risk you took bringing in a key employee who didn't quite measure up, or it could, in fact, be a business failure. I have two clients I'm working with right now, who have been into administration and bankruptcy in previous businesses. Coincidentally, both of them are risk-seekers and are both characterised by strong resilience. I have also been in two partnerships that didn't end well financially and definitely affected the relationship with those partners.

Resilience is an attribute that all business owners need. Two of those business owners that I have worked with and went into administration have picked themselves up, dusted themselves off, and started another business venture as it's in their DNA — it's who they are. On the other hand, one of them has made the decision to go back to the safety and security of fulltime employment.

Henry Ford had two failed automobile businesses before finding success with the Ford Motor Company. Rowland Hussey Macy of department store chain Macy's had two failed retail businesses before the success of Macy's.

What Is Risk, Really?

Very often, the perceived risk of a situation outweighs the actual risk, leading to irrational behaviour. It's worth asking yourself what the worst thing that can happen is and if a business failure is one of those things. For some people, it will be, as their whole being is wrapped up in the business they created. But for most people, you can start over either in business or employment. Just learn from your mistakes, and don't repeat them.

I think this is why we are seeing so many younger people going into business: they're gutsy, some may say, they haven't had to work the way older people have as their parents have attempted to make their lives easier than the lives they had (that's a strong driver for a lot of parents). The younger business owner (millennial, gen Y and X) have less fear partly because their parents have nurtured them and told them they could be whatever they want to be. Also, these younger business owners have formed the view that if something doesn't work, they have enough time to start again, so they give it a crack with far less fear than the older person that fears the loss of their hard-earned assets.

It's really all about how you see risk and where you are in your own life cycle.

How to Be Gutsy?

Guts give business builders the courage to make things happen, stick with it and remain confident no matter the impediments they face.

Guts-driven entrepreneurs aren't fearless; they just know how to cope with and maybe even thrive in uncomfortable environments. They're the same people who crammed for their exams the night before, and often they thrived in high-pressure situations.

Recognise that you already have guts in that you may have already been in business or the fact that you're reading this book means that you're contemplating going into business — that takes guts.

The guts to endure let us recognise that failure is not an option but rather a reality. It's about remaining strong and resolute, persevering in the short term to realise your longer-term goals.

You will experience failure. Expect it, relish it and learn from it.

And for those who are risk-seekers, try to take on characteristics of the risk-tolerators or consider getting one of them to join you in your business. Partnerships aren't easy, but they provide balance and discipline that often the risk-seeker lacks but so desperately needs.

"If you're not a risk taker,
you should get the hell out of business."
—Ray Kroc

"Take calculated risks. Act boldly and thoughtfully.
Be an agile company."
—Ray Kroc

The second aspect of guts in business relates to your intuition or your gut feeling. As you go through the discovery process evaluating franchise opportunities, you will get a feeling — trust it.

Gut Feeling

Have you ever had a feeling in your gut or felt that something just didn't feel quite right? This is referred to as intuition, a combination of our experiences, instinct and senses. Sometimes when you meet someone for the first time, you instinctively sense whether you can trust that person or not. It has been said that women have better intuition than men, but all of us experience intuition or have those gut feelings.

The reason I wanted to include this section is that every time that I have felt something is not quite right or seems too good to be true, my intuition or gut feeling has proven to be right. Sometimes, I have gone with my gut feeling, and other times I have not.

I believe the situation that you're in influences whether you make decisions rationally or emotionally. Don't get me wrong when I say 'emotionally' because that gives the impression that this may be a bad attribute. Sometimes your emotions just make sense, and you should go with them.

I think I'm a good judge of character, but I am also characterised by extreme optimism. I tend to see the best in people and am quite trusting, but at times, I haven't trusted myself and gone with my gut feeling. I've given people or situations the benefit of the doubt. What I've recognised is when I'm stressed or a little desperate, I can make bad decisions. When I'm under duress, I tend not to be as intuitive, and this is probably the time to be more rational.

I believe we need to trust our gut and use our intuition more, but we need to make sure we do it in times when we have a clear mind, free from stress. If you're under pressure, don't dismiss your intuition, but balance it with being more analytical.

Trust your gut instinct; it will usually be right.

CHAPTER 5

WHICH FRANCHISE IS RIGHT FOR ME?

Know thyself to know what you need.

Which Franchise Is Right for Me?

Often when we work with prospective franchisees, people may become fixated on an industry sector or particular concept, and it's not until they fully understand the detail of each opportunity can they fully appreciate the pros and cons of these options. I have a favourite saying in franchising: Don't fall in love with the idea of being a business owner; fall in love with the business model, and make sure it suits what you're trying to achieve by going into business.

Be very clear on what your objectives are for going into business because this will help you determine if you should, in fact, go into business and, if you do, which business is going to help you achieve what you want to achieve.

We do a lot of work with our clients on identifying what the business owners' personal vision is. There's been a lot of discussion on business vision, and this is important for the direction of the business and contribution to its success. But for the business owner, you need to know why you're doing the business, what do you want it to do for you. Stephen Covey wrote in *The 7 Habits of Highly Effective People* that one of the key principles is to start with the end in mind, which basically means know what you want the business to do for you and don't lose sight of that. All too often, business owners get so caught up in their business day-to-day that they lose sight of their 'why'.

Three Types of Business Owners

While there is no single behavioural style or motivator that makes a successful business owner, there are similarities shared by the most successful. John Warrillow, bestselling author of *Built to Sell* and creator of The Value Builder System, has developed three contrasting profiles that provide a simple model for classifying the three most common business owner types.

1. The craftsman is a highly skilled person who creates a business because they know how to create a superior product. The custom motorcycle builder, the donut maker, the smartphone app developer. Their energy is primarily focused on the creation of the product that they provide and less on running and growing a business. Michael Gerber refers to these types of business owners as technicians in his book *The E-Myth*.

2. The mountain climber sees the development of their business as a series of hurdles to cross and a series of peaks to ascend. While they possess a strong drive to succeed, they never find true satisfaction in their work. Each conquered goal is followed by an even loftier one. Once they have created a successful company, they are not content to just run it. Instead, they conquered that challenge — now, on to the next one.

I have to admit to being guilty of this. I have always owned a business while employed on a fulltime basis, and since leaving paid employment, I have had as few as three businesses and as many as seven at any given time. I like building things.

The beauty of my current business, Franchise Ready, is that it has enabled me to harness my need to build businesses by working with other business owners and effectively becoming part of their teams. I have personally coached over 200 business owners in the past eight years, have been their trusted advisor and business coach and have been able to get intimately involved in the development of more than 150 new franchise brands in the past four years. This enables me to quench my first for building successful businesses and moving on to the next project.

I want to comment on the new generation of business owners that I have encountered in the past three years. There is a huge increase in the number of millennial business owners. For instance, out of over 40 business owners I coach at the moment, more than 20 of them are in the late 20s and early 30s. The reason why I mention this is that nearly all of them are 'mountain climbers'. This next generation of business owners are very different to the older and more experienced business owners I work with, who tend to be more like 'craftsmen' and tend to have had their businesses for much longer periods of time (over 15 years). This is compared to the millennial business owners I work with, who want to build, flip, and be out within five years so they can move to the next project.

3. The freedom fighter strives for independence. They have been an employee in other businesses and decided to leave and start their own endeavour. There is no one-size-fits-all freedom fighter, but you might be one if you've ever been a part of a system and thought, 'I can do this better'. It's the freedom fighter's constructive attitude that makes them so unique and makes them perfect for a franchise system.

Whereas craftsmen and mountain climbers will have a strong desire to develop their own concept for a new business, freedom fighters are great fits for owning a franchise system; especially one that combines a framework for success with a lot of flexibility.

The Freedom Fighter in the Franchise System

The freedom fighter is typically utilitarian and individualistic. They often feel that their managers don't know what they're doing and that they could do better. The following statements are reflective of the thoughts of a freedom fighter.

- They've often been sceptical about the decisions that the leaders of companies they worked for have made.
- They've felt frustrated that they don't have enough control over their career and their life.
- They may have believed that if they were in charge, they would approach things differently — and have a better outcome.
- They feel like their skills and their knowledge are often under-utilised by the businesses that they work for.
- They've had the thought in the back of their mind that they'd like to start their own business someday, so that they could benefit from running things their way.
- They've had the desire to have a greater impact on the world.

Success in Freedom

There are two types of franchise systems out there. One type is highly controlling; everything that they do must follow a precise, step-by-step process. For example, if they run a food-related franchise system, they cannot conceptualise new products or deserts nor can they make variations on the set products. The store will look identical to any other franchise operators. They need to operate within a very strict framework that allows zero creativity. This type of system is not too appealing to a freedom fighter.

What's so great about the freedom fighter is that they can operate within a pre-existing system and make it fit their personal vision. They don't necessarily seek freedom from a system or guidelines but freedom to work flexibly.

Even within the three archetypes, you will encounter extroverts and introverts, and franchisors can often be drawn to the extroverted applicant, but extroversion is not a guarantee of success. They may be good talkers but not the best listeners. On the other hand, the introvert may have many attributes that are desirable for franchising. So if you're reading this and thinking business ownership may not be right for you, please read on, you could be just what the franchisor is looking for.

The Introvert

There is a prolific stereotype that in order to be a successful business owner, you have to be a gregarious and assertive extrovert. On the contrary, not only do introverts make great managers, but the unique qualities that introverts possess allow them to excel as leaders in their field. Operating your own franchise requires dedication, commitment and attention to detail, all of which often may be strengths that introverts possess. Below I discuss some such characteristics that may be more often found in introverts and which can be helpful when entering the world of franchising.

Introverts remain calm under pressure.

They are known for remaining level-headed, even in times of high stress. Operating a thriving business is a high-pressure job, and to be successful, excellent stress management is imperative.

Introverts are approachable.

To be a great leader, you need to appear welcoming to your clients and employees. With a calm and collected disposition, introverts naturally put others at ease. This not only enables workplace cohesion but also creates a more open dialogue among staff and enables employees to express their thoughts, questions or concerns more readily.

Introverts are prepared.

Rather than hastily diving into a business meeting or project, they prefer to meticulously plan things out to ensure everything runs smoothly. This not only improves efficiency and effectiveness but it also helps to reduce business risk and eliminate errors.

Introverts are great listeners.

Excellent listening skills are essential in business because they allow the business owner to more effectively understand the needs and wants of both clients and employees. This allows them to correct problems as they occur and to tailor their business practices to better suit client preferences.

Introverts are focused.

Since introverts may prefer solitude, they can remain focused and free of distractions more easily. This facilitates a higher level of productivity in the workplace and assures meticulous attention to detail. Introverts are known for being thinkers who are incredibly thorough and fastidious. This allows them to catch small details that slip by most people.

Introverts are good writers.

Though not always true, many introverts prefer writing over talking, which can provide a serious advantage in the business world. Writing is a constant necessity when operating a company, and clear written communication is critical.

Introverts think things through.

They tend to be less impulsive than extroverts, which is essential when operating a business. Impulsive people engage in higher-risk behaviour that may compromise the finances of a company. Introverts take time to scrupulously assess a situation prior to acting, which greatly minimizes the potential for error and maximizes leadership effectiveness.

Introverts possess excellent leadership qualities that allow them to excel in the business world. Their calm and collected nature allows them to thrive under pressure, and their quiet and amicable temperament makes them more approachable to staff. This enables them to construct business environments with strong teamwork and values that encourage company growth.

So, in summary, it doesn't matter if you're an introvert or an extrovert because both have positives. If you're an extrovert, there's a chance you may make rash or quick decisions and go with your gut, they may be a risk seeker, whilst an introvert is a little more cautious and reflective in their decision-making and may be a risk tolerator. An extrovert can learn from the introvert how to make decisions and approach the challenges of business.

How to Choose the Best Business for You?

Now, it's time to decide what might be the right business for you to choose but with so many, how do you choose? With hundreds of thousands of businesses to choose from, the best place to start is with the industry sector that makes the most sense to you, whether that be a financially driven decision or a pragmatic one based on who you are and what you like.

Here are a few things I'd like you to consider and some terms that I will refer to throughout this section.

Hunter and farmer

The main difference in the hunter versus farmer sales approach is how they each go about generating revenue. The hunter drives revenue by generating interest in their products and services by going out and getting customers and then selling to them. The farmer, on the other hand, generates revenue by nurturing and growing existing customers but tends to wait for the customers to come to them.

A closer

A salesperson goes through the sales process but may not ask for the business and close the sale; a closer does the same but knows when to ask for the business and how to handle objections.

Reactive or proactive

Being reactive means reacting to a situation as it happens, whereas being proactive refers to the anticipation of probable future events and taking action before a future event.

A technician

The technician loves to specialise. For instance, a baker that loves to bake and a painter that loves to paint, are doers and have a technical aptitude for the trade they choose. This is the personality that lives in the present and is happiest when working at one thing at a time, being in control of the workflow.

Extroverted and introverted

A person who remains isolated or enjoys the company of a few close ones and keeps himself busy with thinking is called an introvert. An outgoing and outspoken person who enjoys being around and talking to people is an extrovert. By nature, introverts are self-contained and reserved, whereas extroverts are friendly, talkative and gregarious.

Essentially, extroverts seem to respond better to social cues and rewards, while introverts are more motivated by ideas and internal rewards.

I'll cover these characteristics a little further throughout the book.

So, the first question to ask yourself is what sector to choose. I am going to share with you eight broad industry sectors, each with subsectors or niches for you to consider.

I'll cover these characteristics a little further throughout the book.

So, the first question to ask yourself is what sector to choose. I am going to share with you eight broad industry sectors, each with subsectors or niches for you to consider.

Food Franchise Businesses

When most people hear the word 'franchise', they almost always think of companies like McDonald's, Burger King, KFC, Domino's or Subway because they are the franchise brands with the highest number of outlets globally and after all, we all eat there. Food franchises represent up to 37% of total franchise opportunities globally.

Obviously, food franchises are extremely popular, and they're very recognisable because they invest in marketing their brand and products more than the independent food businesses can and because of the franchise model, they have significant market representation. In other words, you can go most places in the world and find those top five brands I've mentioned above.

In fact, some of the food franchises you see as you're out and about have been around for decades. Of course, some of them are new. Finally, some of them capitalise on the latest trends while others create them.

Starting a Food Franchise Business

Everyone thinks the food business must be successful because there're so many of them.

Most food brands are a franchise but not all of them are available to individuals in some markets as unit franchisees. For instance, Starbucks and Krispy Kreme in Australia are master franchises, but their agreement requires them to operate the brand as company owned, so don't even think you might be able to get your hands on them unless you've got very deep pockets.

People look at food businesses and think they must be good — you don't have to wait for the cash to hit your account like some other franchise opportunities, as they are cash businesses, and the purchase price of the products is usually significantly lower than many other business opportunities. Finally, the cash flow is strong as it flows in daily and most franchisors have negotiated good trading terms with suppliers meaning you don't have to have huge cash tied up in stock.

People think food businesses look easy. After all, we all eat, and lots of us cook food, so it shouldn't be that hard. They look like businesses that practically anyone can operate and make massive amounts of money in. After all, everybody eats and drinks, right? How hard can it be to operate one of these businesses?

The food sector *is* the largest sector in the world of franchising. If you have worked in food service, it's a sector worth investigating if you're looking to buy a franchise. That's because you kind of know what you're in for: it's hard work, you're on your feet for long periods of time and your transaction dollar amount is often low, so you have to get and serve lots of customers.

Some people fall in love with idea of owning a café and having their friends come around. I can assure you it's nothing like that. When you're establishing your food business, you work harder than you've ever worked in your life before. Because it's yours, you have to and, it may take a while to get customers to change their current preferences to your products.

A food franchise would suit any business profile but may be more desirable to the farmer personality or an introvert as once the location is up and running, the owner often waits for customers to come to them. It's true that you should be marketing over and above what your franchisor does, but this may not be your expertise so it tends to be a reactive franchise opportunity.

Some of the negative attributes associated with food franchises include:

- Reliance on team members that are often unskilled and potentially unreliable as they see their role as a stepping stone to their 'real job'.
- Wage costs are wildly variable, and at the whim of sales, it's a fine balancing act. Not too many or labour costs will be too high (ideally 25–30%) and not too low to impact the customer experience. But get this wrong and the results can be catastrophic.
- COGs and labour costs are variable and require excellent controls and recipe management to maintain optimum percentages. Most food businesses need to be under 30% COGs to be profitable.
- It's bloody hard work. Standing on your feet for excessive periods of time, and today, food service is seven days a week from early to late, so it has the potential to impact your quality of life.
- The success of a food business is heavily reliant on real estate: location is everything, and that comes at a price. Ideally, a food business would like to run at 4–10% for full-service restaurants and 8-14% for takeaway, known as quick-service restaurants (QSRs).
- Consumer behaviour can change, and unless you have a strong loyalty program, ongoing marketing and a great product that is always evolving, customers are prone to try other products.
- If you're situated in a shopping centre and to a lesser degree on a high street, there's a strong chance of competition and copying of your best products which you have no control over.

I started my career working in food and have over 40 years of experience owning and operating food businesses, including the four that I own right now. I have a love–hate relationship with food businesses because they can be great but they can also be very hard work. I've made it harder on myself because I own multiple businesses, but that's the power of franchising: you run the systems and the people run the business. So, you need to get into a food business that has great systems and then recruit, train, motivate and develop the right people as they will determine the success of your food business as much as you, if not more, as they interact with more customers than you will and will make more products than you, too.

Other Franchise Sectors

Retail

The non-food retail market represents 25% of franchise systems in Australia and is similar in other global franchise communities, these non-food retail businesses are mostly bricks-and-mortar location-based businesses. A large portion of retail business is done online and this has the potential to negatively impact a retail franchise unless it has a dedicated online retail strategy and that you as a franchisee can benefit from it.

The negative aspects of retail franchises include:

- Significant move to online retailing, which adds convenience to the customer journey and removes the need to go in-store to purchase items that are not size dependent.
- Just like food, retail has extremely high leasing costs due in part to landlords not adjusting the rental expectations downward since the 2020 pandemic and increased online retail spending.

- Labour costs are lower than food retail because the product is already produced but can vary greatly, if sales are down due to external factors like weather or special events.
- Shrinkage is higher than in food-related retail businesses as people help themselves to products without paying for them, and the profit margin and COGs are significantly higher, so they can erode profitability.

The retail sector is also a reactive sector waiting for consumers to come to you and can suit either the extrovert or introvert. You will need to evaluate the type of interaction that the customer of that business will want to determine if it is the right business for you. For example, if you owned a bookstore, you are more likely to be a little more introverted, whereas someone working in women's fashion may need to be more upbeat and extroverted in their sales approach and motivating their teams.

The Business-to-business (B2B) Franchise Sector

This is often referred to as the white-collar franchise and suits people coming from corporate life, looking to use their corporate experience to do something for themselves. The key success factor with these types of business is confidence and an ability to sell: you must know and believe in the product and what it does for your buyer. Many B2B franchisors will train you in sales but selling professional services is one of the toughest sectors to get into if you're not a hunter-type personality.

Having launched and physically run six professional services businesses myself, I think, ideally, you have had extensive experience in this space, you must be a hunter and you have to be able to demonstrate the value that your service brings. I have worked in most of the typical professional services sector opportunities in the market, having run an accounting practice, a coaching business, two recruitment businesses and a consulting services business with my current business, Franchise Ready.

All of these services, except the accounting practice, are what I would call 'Value-Added' or 'Optional' businesses for the consumer. Namely, they may need them, but they can operate just fine without them, so you have to demonstrate the value that you bring. This means you have to be good at sales, but then you also have to be good at the areas of your practice. In the coaching business I was in, I observed people that were brilliant coaches and could add enormous value to their clients, but they struggled with sales and closing, so they never had enough clients to have a scalable business. Instead, what they did have was loyal customers that stayed with them for a long time. Then, there's the salesman that loves the thrill of the chase and closing a deal but may not be the best coach unless they are coaching in sales. It's a weird dichotomy in professional services as it requires both left-brain and right-brain skills. Don't get me wrong — this can be learnt. When I worked in recruitment, I was terribly uncomfortable making cold calls to get business but superb at finding what the candidate and client were looking for. Eventually, I got better over time. Then, when I started out as a business coach not only did I have an inferiority complex/imposter syndrome because I did not believe that I knew enough about business or, more specifically, the clients' business that I was approaching, so I struggled with both the sales process and the coaching. But, like riding a bike, you get better with practice, and today I am very confident in both the sales and execution functions of my business.

These are skills that you can learn, but it will not be as quickfire as starting a food or retail business where customers will walk in the door. In this case, you must go out and get them and then be really good at servicing them or they will go elsewhere.

I believe these are the hardest franchises to operate but the most rewarding when and if you get it right. In my coaching franchise system, only 20% of the franchisees would get it right and live the life they dreamt of, whilst the rest struggled for a wage that was lower than their professional career role, with many leaving their practice after three years. But the interesting thing is that when it clicks into gear, it's very rewarding personally and financially. I went from having eight clients each paying me $500 a month to 52 clients paying me $1,000 a month or more.

You need to be confident and instil confidence in your clients in order for them to buy from you. In all of the professional service franchises that I have been involved in, you have to be able to close a deal. I see all too many salespeople perfect their pitch but not read the customer and know when to close and actually ask for the business. I won't go into that here as that is a whole other book on how to sell.

Professional service franchises are the cheapest to get into and have the highest average profit percentage return but they're also the hardest businesses to get right because of the balance needed between hunting, selling, closing and delivering. It can be learnt but will probably take longer to perfect than any other franchise opportunity.

Accommodation

Hotel and motel franchises are the most expensive types of franchises to invest in. Although they may appear glamorous from the outside, hotels trade 24 hours a day, so if something goes wrong overnight, you may find yourself on site more than you'll find yourself at home. In fact, one of my franchise partners in the coaching franchise who moved into a hotel franchise was basically living on site the whole time, taking turns to be on call.

Every market is competitive today, and in the hotel space, the online platforms and discount sites are competing for you and against you. It's a cut-throat industry often driven by price. Whilst it's true you don't have COGs like retail and food operators, your highest costs are labour, servicing the borrowings on the large investment that you have made in the physical plant and the amount of marketing required to get customers to come to you. The average occupancy in hotels in Australia is similar to other countries, and it has fluctuated in recent times due to the pandemic. Prior to the pandemic, hotel occupancy rates sat above 80% and then dropped to below 40%. As I write this, they have come back to just over 60%, and we're on track to get back to pre-pandemic numbers in the 2023/24 season.

The only challenge with that is that the advent and prevalence of online communications and remote work have reduced the need for people to travel, and recent surveys of company CEOs show that companies will spend less on travel and accommodation.

The average profitability in the hotel sector sits at around 30%, so it can be very lucrative, but it is very capital intensive.

There are four sectors that have boomed in recent years, and assuming that the sector suits your style and objectives, they should be considered. They are home services, wellness sector, aged care and anything to do with children.

Home Services

Often referred to as the blue-collar franchise sector, the work can be menial, manual and very hands-on and requires multiple skills, including the need to close a deal and be sales focused but could easily suit an introvert. This type of business requires a hunter mentality to go out and get the work and then the precision of a technician because your customer is engaging you because they may not have the skill to complete the task they are employing you to do.

Consumers today have changed the way they think and act with regard to their homes and leisure time. The pandemic meant more people were at home and seeing all the things that needed improvement, this coupled with a desire to live their life and not physically complete the chores they don't enjoy has resulted in an explosion of home services.

A home services business owner would typically be a 'one-man band' which would suit people that didn't want to manage teams and was happy to be by themselves. The downside of this type of operation is that if you're not working, then you're not generating an income. I often refer to this as buying yourself a job, but on the positive side, you're the boss and you work when you want to.

Often, the home services franchisee is handy and skilled but may lack the business skills required to grow a services business. And this is where a franchise provides the training and support to assist you in the administrative and sales function whilst you leverage your technical skills. I have to say I'm hopeless at anything to do with repairs or handyman-type work, so home services are brilliant for me.

There are hundreds of business opportunities in this space, and many franchisors may offer an income guarantee because they know they can get the work as soon as they turn on the marketing.

I recently heard Jim Penman from Jim's Group of home services business talk about the success rates in the home services sector, and the numbers were staggering. Independent home services businesses have a 90% failure rate in the first year compared to an 88% success rate with a franchise home services business within his group, what this says to me is that if you want to go into home services, a franchise is a must.

The investment level is often the lowest of all franchise opportunities in the market, with a return on your investment in the first 6–12 months. There are limitations on the size of your business in home services, and this is dictated by the size of your territory and whether you scale the business with employees. Unlike food and retail businesses that might sell for two–three times EBITDA, a home service s business may only sell for one–two times EBITDA.

Children's Sector — It's Child's Play

Imagine having 380,000 more customers coming into your marketplace every year, with an existing marketplace made up of over five million existing customers.

In Australia, over 300,000 babies are born each year, whilst New Zealand welcomes over 60,000 new babies each year. Add to this the migration of children into these two countries of over 20,000, and this is an ever-growing market. Australia and New Zealand are enormous markets in terms of the children's sector.

Australia has a population of 27 million people, and New Zealand — a population of over 5 million. Imagine how big the market opportunity is in other parts of the world, especially Asia, where there is significantly more focus on education than in Australia and New Zealand.

It's often said that any business that services the children's products and services sector is a good one to be associated with. Some corporates come under criticism for marketing their products and services to this sector, and some will blame parents for the choices they make when it comes to their children.

Thankfully, the franchise sector has taken a responsible approach to creating business opportunities within this sector and, in so doing, has supported parents and their decision-making and provided invaluable products and services to benefit children.

Within our business at Franchise Ready, we are fortunate to work across all industry sectors and are proud to have launched and supported over 200 brands to grow through franchising, but those that give us the greatest sense of pride and satisfaction are those that make a difference in the lives of children. Providing excellent quality products and services to children just makes sense. After all, what parent doesn't want the best for their children?

"The question is not whether we can afford to invest in every child; it is whether we can afford not to".
Marian Wright Edelman

When we look at this sector and specifically the clients that we work with that have an offering in this sector, we are fortunate to have clients and brands that service children and their families from birth through adolescence. The clients that we work with follow the adage of Benjamin Franklin: 'Tell me and I forget, teach me and I remember, involve me and I learn'. That is the key to engaging children and helping them to love the activities that they undertake, do this, and you should have a sound business.

It Starts at the Beginning

The most important years in a child's development are said to be from birth to the age of five. Children's experiences and relationships that are formed during these years determine how their brain develops. In fact, by the time children reach age five, 90% of a child's brain is already developed. Preschool is the perfect place for your child to build the connections needed for healthy development and a successful future.

For many families, having their children attend childcare or early learning centres provides the perfect environment for developmental growth, but many of these centres have very little substance to their curriculum or pedagogy as it is known within the early childhood sector.

As parents, we have an expectation that these carers will do just that, provide high-quality care to our children — this should be a given. There is one organisation in the market that does so much more than this, MindChamps Early Learning and Preschool programme.

MindChamps started as a research centre in Sydney in 1998 before taking their findings to Singapore — one of the most demanding educational systems in the world — to measure their unique teaching and learning approach against the traditional models.

The MindChamps' distinguishing factor is their dedication to helping each child realise and unlock their true potential by teaching them learning foundations and the love of learning.

An early-education business is financially rewarding with significant government subsidies that make childcare more affordable for all families, which assists with optimising occupancy and ultimately — profitability. All business owners want the opportunity to build equity in an asset that can be sold at some point in the future. The beauty of the childcare sector is that the business value multiples of earnings is higher than every other franchise opportunity in the market, so not only does a business owner do 'good' but they have a very 'good' business.

The industry is heavily regulated, which it needs to be; after all, they are looking after our children, and there is nothing we wouldn't do for our children, so not everyone can enter this sector, but for those that do, it is very rewarding.

The Formative Years

The formative years or the early stages of childhood fall between 0–8 Years of a child's school life, when they learn more quickly than at any other time in life. These are the years in which a child experiences rapid cognitive (intellectual), social, emotional and physical development.

It is estimated that the average Australian and New Zealand child will spend 15–20 hours per week on some form of screen device, whether that be television or other technology. This can be frustrating for parents, so any business that can tear children away from these devices to engage in activities that will stimulate their children socially, emotionally, physically and intellectually has a strong chance of receiving a parent's blessing. But in order to convert this into a successful business, it needs to engage the child and make them want to continue with that brand, product or service; ultimately, it has to be enjoyable.

Five of our clients have successfully achieved this. They have made their products and services fun whilst addressing children's social, emotional, physical and intellectual needs. The services that they offer complement the foundations that MindChamps lays in those first five years.

Ninja Kids

Ninja Kids is the home of Australia's most loved ninja warrior–style gym for kids. Its mission is to get children out of the house and into physical activity because a physically active child is a healthy child.

Physical activity strengthens a child's muscles and bones, prevents excessive weight gain and reduces the risk of diabetes, cancer and other conditions. Physical activity is also beneficial to the mental health of a child, and experts say physical activity allows children to have a better outlook on life by building confidence, managing anxiety and depression, and increasing self-esteem and cognitive skills.

Some children try team sports but may not be cut out for it, while Ninja Kids is designed for every child. No matter their skill level, every child has the chance to participate and better their previous best self. Whilst they may be working individually, they are also working within a group, so the benefits socially are enormous. Ninja Kids offers regular programme, school holiday camps and birthday parties and is consistently in demand. It's a solid business opportunity with benefits for the children that attend and provides some respite for their parents all the time, knowing that their children are in good hands, having fun and learning key skills that will benefit them in all aspects of their life.

Stormer Music

Have you ever noticed that the kids that did music in school also happened to be the smartest kids in school? There are significant benefits to engaging with music and the impact that it has on children and their development. Studies in neuroscience show that music can enhance brain function in children. Musical activities (such as playing an instrument, singing or just listening to music) stimulate the brain, and this brain workout leads to improved brain structure with the formation of new neural connections. Music can help improve memory, attention and concentration, coordination, achievements and discipline.

All great benefits, but what's even better is there's now an opportunity for musicians and music lovers to make a business out of it. Stormer Music is a family business with generations of musos coming together to bring music to the world in a franchise format and with nine locations up and running, they're making beautiful music together.

Stormer Music was created by Joel and Phil Stormer, musicians with a love of music and education, who incorporated their passion into a business to complement their music career and booking agency business. In sum, this is a story of people creating a business out of something they love.

Skill Samurai

We already established that children are spending way too much time on screen devices and a lot of time on gaming and computers. Skill Samurai is helping kids channel their obsession with technology into expanding their knowledge instead of simply distracting them or entertaining them.

Skill Samurai provides after-school and school holiday programmes for children and teaches them coding and essential computer skills that will benefit them well into the future. Future programs are being launched to target the development of IT-related work and preparing students for careers within the IT sector.

Skill Samurai turns a fixation with technology into a practical, educational and fun outlet with tangible educational benefits for children whilst having fun.

Success Tutoring

There are so many tutoring services available for primary and high school students; the difference with Success Tutoring lies in their mission of motivating, uplifting and inspiring students to enjoy learning.

The educational model is research backed, using an 'inspired-learning' teaching method. This method suggests that inspired students are more attentive and engaged in their lessons, which correlates with an improvement in their academic performance and grades — that's the Success Tutoring's difference.

As the only tutoring company that uses motivation to unlock students' maximum academic potential, Success Tutoring's impact extends far beyond the four walls of a classroom by transforming students into active life learners. They understand that the traditional, one-size-fits-all approach to learning limits the academic potential of some students. Success Tutoring tailors each lesson to the immediate needs and characteristics of the student.

Tutors curate a lesson plan that facilitates the basic psychological need for competence, connection and autonomy to achieve academic success in accordance with the principles of the self-determination theory.

This business was created by an 18-year-old entrepreneur who had a vision of revolutionising the education sector, Michael Black. Together with a couple of school mates, Black created something special for school-aged children by identifying the gaps in their own educational journey and wanting to give every student the best opportunity at school and beyond. We had the pleasure to work with Michael in developing his brand and I was super proud when Michael was recognised in the Australian Top 30 Franchise Executives in 2022 — a testament to what he has created with Success Tutoring and how he and his team are changing the tutoring sector.

Every business needs to make money, and it needs to stand for something. The beauty of the children's products and services category is that what it does resonates with us all: we can all relate to our own experiences of growing up, the highs and the lows and as the carers, families and parents of children and we all want the best for our children. We want them to have all the positive attributes we enjoyed in our childhood, protect them from the things we didn't enjoy and give them the best chance at life. And if we can do that in a way that they enjoy, everyone wins.

So not only are these good businesses, but they also do good.

Wellness — Health, Fitness, Personal Care and Beauty

Health, fitness and beauty may be the sector headings, but the outcome is wellness and never has this been more in the spotlight than since the pandemic of 2020. There has been considerable discussion in the media about the impact that the pandemic had on our mental health. A significant proportion of Australians experienced lower levels of wellbeing, higher levels of psychological distress, long periods of loneliness and social isolation.

Many of us even joked about our 'Covid bodies', and Covid not being kind to our health, fitness and beauty regime, but at the same time, there has been a significant increase in the use of social media as a way to connect during those periods of social distancing and isolation.

Coming out the other side, we have seen a rapid uptake in the number of wellness services being used, and within the franchise sector, several new entrants focused on helping people feel better about themselves.

Some parts of the population have been impacted financially, both positively through government support and negatively through reduced working hours and income. But the common theme among both sides of the financially impacted is the desire to focus on their own wellbeing, looking after themselves more and treating themselves in a healthier way.

During lockdown, many of these services took a beating, but they are coming back strong, and the general population is embracing the need to look after themselves better and treat themselves in a healthier way and this has given rise to the early stages of a booming sector, and there's never been a better time to get into a business within this wellness category.

Mental health is a key component of overall health and wellbeing, according to the WHO data from 2013. More recently, there has been a significant increase in mental health issues brought about by Covid-19 and the associated impact of restrictions that were implemented. There is no better representation than observing the significant increase in MBS-subsidised mental health-related services that were processed between 16 March 2020 and 9 January 2022, with almost 25 million services processed.

The government has done a good job by investing more funds into this sector, but the general population has also recognised the need to look after themselves better and this is where we are seeing the surge in the use of the wellness sector.

Reinvention is the key for every business in this new post-pandemic world because what worked pre-Covid may not necessarily work in this new world. Businesses must change their model and services to maintain relevance and open new potential markets focused on improving overall wellness for a broader market. After all, we have all been impacted by this pandemic and the fallout from it.

Fitness and Health

The fitness industry was decimated during Covid and had to pivot to an online business model until the market opened back up. This has changed the fitness space significantly, whilst many gyms did not make it. Those that did were those that reinvented themselves by creating pandemic-proof businesses and doing fitness more holistically.

Beginning with the baby boom generation, more people have come to understand the importance of lifelong fitness and have devoted themselves to staying in shape. Additionally, awareness of the role of nutrition in overall health and wellness has been growing.

New franchises that combine fitness education and training with nutritional counselling and product sales are beginning to gain popularity among the public looking for help in its quest for optimal health.

There are over 8,000 gyms in Australia and New Zealand, with over 32% of the population having a gym membership and nearly 50% of the population participating in regular exercise. We know there's a demand for fitness and health-related offerings. We have seen the meteoric rise of functional fitness and 24/7 gyms, so to get cut through in this sector, operators need to differentiate themselves and take this sector to a new level.

One of our clients has decided to focus on the quality of service rather than the once popular budget 24/7 gym models. Fit Clinic is the brainchild of exercise physiologist Aaron King. Aaron has created a 'gym that's not a gym' where degree-qualified exercise physiologists are on hand in the studio to deliver advice around technique and a scientific approach to individual wellness goals through personalised programs delivered through one-to-one, group and open gym sessions where members can receive a follow-up on their personalised programs and objectives.

Fitillion is the brainchild of Mike Kunitz who has created Australia's newest and most innovative gym franchise. Fitillion introduces personalised team training to both the studio and the home gym environments. Each member receives customised workouts for their skill level and fitness goal, as well as a tailored meal plan with recipes and shopping lists or home-delivered meals. To stay on track with their fitness goal and body transformation journey, each member receives a Fitillion home smart scale, which provides industry-leading accuracy for body fat and muscle mass readings.

Another of our clients, CHANGƎ, has set about to change the fitness and wellbeing industry. Pete Haselhurst and Emma-Jean Pearson, who came out of the once successful F45 business owning as many as eight studios, could see that fitness needed to change and take on a more holistic approach. CHANGƎ has leveraged the best of all the fitness options in the market by having a functional fitness gym with yoga and meditation and Reformer Pilates studio under one roof, consolidating the three most popular wellbeing options with one membership.

If you're going into this sector, you need to learn from the past, embrace the current and look to the future and ensure a well-balanced approach to overall wellness.

Whilst this sector can be expensive to set up and ramping up membership a challenge in a very competitive market, once you establish a brand in this sector it is extremely lucrative with low labour costs and no COGs and profit margins upwards of 40%.

Personal Care and Beauty

With the continued rise of social media, image is becoming important, but more importantly, we all deserve a little pampering, the ability to take some time out and do something for ourselves. Google Search Trends shows a 250% increase in self-care-related searches. Men and women of all age ranges believe that self-care is an important part of making healthier lifestyle choices, and many of them believe that self-care practices have an impact on their overall wellbeing.

Whether it's a mobile nail salon like Nail Call founded by Heidi Powrie who brings the experience to homes and workplaces or the self-tanning phenomenon of Tan Lounge founded by Charley Costin, offering a subscription model where you can get an affordable and amazing tan whenever you want — that's right 24/7 for one low subscription monthly cost.

'In a country where one of the leading cancers is skin cancer, providing a space for people to get their bronze on without the life-damaging effects is one of the things I'm incredibly passionate about. At Tan Lounge, we pride ourselves on being inclusive for all body types, all genders and all occupations. We see people from all walks of life come through our doors, whether they're a mum, working in corporate, modelling and acting or even a tradie — each one finds something important in their tanning routine, each one feels better walking out than when they did walking in. And it is so much more than a tan,' says Charley.

Personal care franchises like spas, beauty salons and massage therapy centres are seeing rapid growth by bringing the cost of pampering yourself down to a level that average people can afford. As franchises like one of our newly franchised clients, Jun Lin Spa, become a staple in most cities, franchisees are branching out even more into niche markets that serve growing needs.

The story of founder Van Truong is truly inspirational. In her business, she has combined an Eastern approach to the benefit of the Western world by creating salons that pamper by incorporating beauty services with massage therapy in one location. (I'm going to try and get her to write a book about it, as she blows my mind with what she has achieved.)

Personal grooming businesses like barbershops and another of our clients, Pores X, created by livewire Rachel Ng, service the skin care market for the male population, making skin treatments easy, affordable and fast.

Services that used to be available only at exclusive day spas that cost hundreds of dollars and took an entire day can now be enjoyed on your lunch hour for a fraction of the cost. Pores X target young males and the male market, offering them a subscription model for skincare that can be delivered within 15 minutes in the convenience of your local shopping centre, removing the stigma around men going to traditional beauty salons.

The key to success in this wellness sector is being innovative and holistic in your approach to the wellbeing of people. The most successful businesses and franchises are those that recognise that these once standalone sectors now need to be integrated and that health and fitness, personal care and beauty are all linked, and those that can incorporate them into one business model stand the best chance of success. That's not to say that you can't have a standalone, niche business within the sector, but if you do, you need to do it better than anyone else.

Home Care

There has been significant growth in government expenditure for home care services, which correlates with a 24% increase year on year of people receiving home care services. As of June 2021, there were 906 providers delivering home care services in Australia, a significant increase since 2016, when there were 487 providers.

This large increase can be attributed to government reforms that reduced barriers to entry, additional home care funding and the introduction of consumer choice in home care. Of these providers, 80% are not-for-profit providers and 20% are private providers.

On 30 June 2022, approximately 407,000 people were using residential aged care, home care or transition care in Australia. This comprises 188,000 people using permanent or respite residential aged care, 216,000 using home care and 3,500 using transition care. In addition, during the 2021–22 period, over 818,000 people were assisted under the Commonwealth Home Support Programme (Home Support). The market is huge and will continue to increase as our population ages.

It is an industry that takes in over $20 billion in revenue in Australia and employs over 250,000 people across the country. Despite a decline in demand for residential aged care, the Australian aged care market continues to grow, largely due to an increase in home care, and this is where the opportunity exists for franchising.

Entry into this sector is low cost with high potential return because of the strong demand.

National Disability Insurance Scheme (NDIS)

The NDIS was created by the federal government to support a better life for hundreds of thousands of Australians with a significant and permanent disability and their families and carers. To this end, the NDIS provides funding to eligible people with disability to gain more time with family and friends, greater independence, access to new skills, jobs or volunteering in their community and improved quality of life. The NDIS also connects anyone with a disability to services in their community. This includes connections to doctors, community groups, sporting clubs, support groups, libraries and schools, as well as providing information about what support is provided by each state and territory government.

The NDIS now supports over 500,000 Australians with disability to access the services and supports they need. This includes supporting approximately 80,000 children with developmental delay, ensuring they receive supports early so that they achieve the best outcomes throughout their lives.

Entry into this sector is low cost, but the industry is highly regulated and getting a licence as an approved provider of the NDIS services can be difficult unless you have the requisite qualifications. Joining a franchise business that has developed the systems and processes and has the licences makes entry into this sector a little easier with government funding which has been increasing every year.

The sector is booming, and there is a shortage of qualified support workers and businesses providing the services that are required, just like the children's sector there is immense good in supporting this sector.

How to Decide?

When identifying a franchise opportunity that you are interested in pursuing, it is important to go through an evaluation process to determine whether the opportunity has a good chance of being successful. A franchise is a business prospect that should not be entered lightly. Taking time to research and plan will pay dividends through the length of your franchise term, however long that may be.

So, regardless of what your profile, if you're considering being a franchisee, make sure that you select the right franchise to suit you and check with the franchisor about the rigidity of their system and make sure that their model suits you and what you are looking get to out of business ownership.

As business owners, we go too often into business with a vision, but we can get lost in the detail of what we do every day. This will happen to you, so it's imperative that the business you settle on satisfies your every need and the only way to know that is a thorough investigation, your research is important but just as important is your gut feeling.

The right franchise for you is the one that feels right.

CHAPTER 6

DOES SIZE MATTER?

It's all relative

We always say to our clients, 'We're going to challenge you to "think bigger" than you've dared to dream, but it's important that it's within your ability to manage'. That's the beauty of franchising — the business model has been developed for you; your role is to work the business model to achieve your objectives.

We're not irresponsible when we tell people to think big because sometimes, we must temper people's enthusiasm for the size of business they want to run or whether they could do it in the first place.

I often hear founders and CEOs of franchise brands claiming to open 100, 500 or 1,000 outlets. It sounds good in the press, but the reality is there needs to be a very good business model to support that growth and a clear strategy on how to get there. This is just as important for the single-unit franchisee as it is for franchise brands that aspire to be much bigger.

There are two aspects of the size that I'd like to share with you in this chapter: the size and maturity of the franchise brand you're considering and the size of the operation that you want to run yourself.

One of the most common questions we get asked by business owners that want to franchise their business is 'Do I have to be a certain size in order to franchise?'. That could refer to revenue or location numbers, and although this may help potential franchisees make a decision, it's more about the quality of the business opportunity and the business model. We see great small businesses, businesses with only one location, and they can be amazing, and, on the flipside, we see large businesses that are just not good.

The single-unit 'husband and wife team' arrangement may be what most people think of when they think about franchise ownership. In Australia and New Zealand, this is by far the biggest part of the franchise market, and for some people, buying into a franchise is buying themselves a job to support their family and to be their own boss. This is a perfect model for those that can't or don't want to create something from scratch and all the risk that goes with that. As we established earlier, the franchise success rate is much higher than independent businesses, but there is still a risk of failure in franchising.

The premise of franchising is that an owner/operator will do a better job than an employee — that was Ray Kroc's (founder of modern-day McDonald's) approach when he started franchising. Initially, he allowed investors to own McDonald's restaurants, but what he found was that operationally they weren't as strong as owner-operated restaurants. McDonald's still refer to their franchisees as owners/operators because there's an expectation that they work in and on the business.

Interesting that today, it is common practice for McDonald's operators to have 10 plus stores in Australia, and internationally, there are operators with over 100 restaurants. Internationally, this is much more common.

I was at the International Franchise Association convention in San Diego in 2022, and I was excited to hear Shaquille O'Neal talk (because I'm a massive basketball fan). I used to think he had fallen on hard times because he was doing so many TV commercials; what I now know is he has been strategic in building his personal brand but also in leveraging other brands in his vast business portfolio. At one time, he owned 155 Five Guys hamburger restaurants and invested in Krispy Kreme, forty 24 Hour Fitness centres, Papa John's, 17 Auntie Anne's Pretzels franchises and 150 car washes. He has also started his own chicken brand that now has more than 35 restaurants. Why do I share that with you? Because it demonstrates the power of franchising. Shaq likes eating hamburgers and chicken, but that's not his skill set. Instead, through leveraging franchising and a proven business model, he has built an empire.

Now you may be content with a single franchise operation, but if you aspire for more, franchising provides the platform to do so. I can speak from personal experience. Until recently, I was invested in five franchises as a franchisee, but I was a bad franchisee as I didn't work in any of them. They still made money but underperformed because they didn't have the proprietorial element driving the performance of the business. Now, had they been independent businesses, they may have all failed because they didn't have the systems in place to support an absentee owner.

I believe you need to start with one and do it well and then move on to the next opportunity, which could be within the same brand (which does make it easier) or by investing in multiple brands and potentially spreading your risk and satisfying your potential need for diversity.

If you have the financial security, operational experience and motivation to own multiple businesses, align yourself with franchise brands that embrace multi-unit operators. A lot of franchisors like this model because these operators tend to be more business minded than the technician personalities who like to ply their trade and focus on doing one thing well. With multi-unit franchisees, the franchisor gets to deal with fewer people, which makes their ability to communicate and support those multi-unit franchisees better.

But there are other franchise ownership structures that assist with rapid expansion. These larger, more complicated organisations require a sophisticated, seasoned business approach. The demands and risks can be greater, but so are the returns.

The Area Developer

There are multiple definitions of an 'area developer'. Sometimes it's used as a catch-all to describe franchisees who take on the additional responsibility of recruiting, training and supporting other franchisees. For this service, they claim a percentage of the franchise fee and royalty. When I was in The Alternative Board, this was a role they used in remote regions of the USA and Canada, but only with the most successful franchise partners, and these individuals didn't get that role from the start. They had to demonstrate their ability to do more whilst still running a successful unit franchise business.

In the context of this description, we define area developers as having the rights to develop franchise units in an exclusive territory and agreeing to open a number of units by a specific date. Failing to do so imposes penalties, usually financial, including the loss of exclusivity or the loss of the deal entirely. Negotiations, however, are common, and economic climates often dictate terms.

There are benefits to both the franchisee and franchisor with area developers and multi-site franchisees: the talent pool is greater, the impact of losing key personnel is lessened in the area developer model, training and communications are easier. It's more efficient to interact with one entity opening 15 units than with 15 single-unit owners.

Larger Territories and Master Franchising

When a franchise system grants a master franchise their goal is expansion into a larger territory, usually a whole state or, quite often, another country. The master franchisee, with their local knowledge, contacts, and networks, takes on the entire responsibility normally handled by the franchise system. Master franchisees sell, recruit, train and support franchisees throughout the territory acquired.

There are benefits to both the franchisor and master franchisee. The franchisor gets to grow an often-remote market more quickly and cost-effectively than doing it themselves, whilst that master franchisee gets a proven system and known brand that often can easily absorb into existing infrastructure. It can be the perfect partnership where each party uses the other's money to grow.

Selecting the right master franchisee is critical. The capital requirements are significant, the challenges and responsibilities are exponentially greater than for area developers. Keen management skills and a proven organisation, either in place or a demonstrated track record of developing something similar, are essential. One must also have a deep understanding of sales, marketing and business operations, and it helps to have experience in franchising.

Experience in franchising, however, while desirable, is not an absolute as the franchisor is there for support. International marketing, access to the latest systems and technologies and an open door to the highest levels of the organisation all accrue to the master franchisee's benefit. For those possessing the right attributes — financial wherewithal, existing business infrastructure, sales and marketing experience, connections with financial institutions within the prescribed territory — master franchising offers the most potential for accelerated growth for both the franchisor and the master franchisee.

We use franchise industry-specific behavioural profiling to determine the capabilities of franchisees which highlights their potential aptitude for bigger operations, but a demonstrable track record of success running a larger business, growing it and leading a larger team can be a good guide to the potential of a prospect. After all, the franchisor has done it before and part of their role is to mentor and support their master franchisees.

Emerging or Established Franchise Business

Just because a franchise brand is new to franchising doesn't mean that their business is new. To franchise a business, there must be a proven business model that has worked and that can be replicated. These emerging franchise brands may have perfected their operations and business model, but they will typically not have experience as franchisors unless they have been employed in sophisticated franchise brands before. This means they will be learning as they go — this is good and bad. Good because they will work with you, and together, you can grow the brand and there may be more flexibility than in a more established franchise brand. It could be bad because they haven't done it before, and running a franchise system is very different from running the business that got them to franchise. There is a unique skill set required to be a franchisor and not everyone can do it.

There are several factors to consider with an emerging franchise: the brand, consumer preferences, support, experience and profitability.

- What is the brand?
- What does it stand for?
- Do consumers have that product or service in their consideration set?
- How competitive is the market?
- How are they perceived in the market? (More on this in the branding chapter of this book, but often, emerging franchise brands have less awareness to consumers than more established brands.)
- Do customers like or need the product or service on offer?
- What research has the franchisor done on market demand in the area that you are considering?

I know this is a different example, but I remember when we took an Australian brand to America in 2003 and failed, the reason it failed other than the obvious of not doing adequate research was to do with the product we had. In Australia, 70% of our business was done before 11 am with that product in shopping centres, and in the USA, the shopping centres didn't open until 10 am and closed at 10 pm, and our product did not suit that market or daypart.

Also, consider the support aspect:

- Who is in the franchisor support team?
- How are they going to support you especially if you are situated a distance from the support office?

- Do they have their supply chain set up in other territories? (So you can deliver the same products.)
- What experience does the franchisor and their support team have in franchising and growing and supporting a franchise? (Often, newer franchise concepts will see early adopter franchisees receive significantly more support because the franchisor needs them to be successful to grant/sell more franchises.)

The key question to be answered is the financial aspect of the new business, especially if it has not been franchised before so you don't have access to the financials of other franchisees. Sometimes, the franchisor can run a more profitable business unit because they have perfected that, and some new franchisees may find it harder to achieve the results that the franchisor has achieved, you also need to understand the impact that franchise fees have on the overall profitability as these are often not shown in the franchisor corporate model.

Starting a new business takes guts and patience at any time, but trusting an unproven franchise model can be even riskier than a franchise model that's been around for a while because you just don't have the track record of performance to compare to.

Investing in any business is a true measure of your intestinal fortitude and patience, but this may even ring truer when considering an emerging franchise. The first 36 months of a new business takes perseverance, a willingness to work harder than you've ever worked before (likely for less money), a true belief in yourself and a lot of confidence in yourself and the brand. With an up-and-coming franchise, you are riding out the growth of a new brand in addition to the growth of a new business which can present a whole new set of growing pains. Because these franchise systems are typically smaller and there isn't as much history, there are more unknowns. But that may not necessarily be a bad thing and may even be the reason a franchisee is drawn to a new concept in the first place.

It's important to remember that just because a brand has existed longer, that doesn't necessarily mean it's better. Getting in on the ground floor with a newer concept offers benefits that may not be available with a more established brand, such as the opportunity to secure larger territories and more locations, paying lower startup fees and being able to take part in shaping the brand as it grows.

Newer franchise brands tend to be a little more relevant to the current market than a brand that may have been around for a long time. Sometimes legacy brands are difficult to change operationally and even more so in the minds of the consumer.

Below are listed the critical things to review when considering an emerging franchise. Make sure they have invested in the development of their systems and that the business blueprint is well documented so that you can pick it up and run with it.

Business Model

Make sure you fully understand how the franchisor is going to help you and how is their business model designed to ensure an optimum chance of success. This is covered in a lot of detail in the next chapter. This is the 'how to' make money and a fair return on your investment.

Ask to see their financial reports and review the disclosure document to see how they are performing. The challenge with an emerging brand is that they do not have to include their financials for the first two years of operating the franchise.

If there are other franchisees in the network, you should ask them about the business model, the KPIs and the financial performance of the business. If existing franchisees doesn't disclose the numbers, that could be a red flag.

Financial Position of the Franchisor

The franchise system needs to be well capitalised (beyond royalty collection) to fund the growth of the system long term. In the same way that you need a healthy cash reserve to get through lean days, so should the franchisor. Lack of capital usually means a younger brand's ability to grow quickly may be severely compromised.

Advertising and Marketing

A franchisor's ability to bring the brand to life involves much more than trademarks and taglines. It's important that the franchisor is committed to building their new brand through professional advertising and marketing campaigns. You'll want to find out what types of campaigns have been deployed and ensure that the materials are being professionally developed. Ask whether the campaigns have been tested and what kind of returns operating units are seeing. This is covered in a lot more detail in the brand chapter of this book.

Operational Processes and Manuals

Ask to see the operational manuals as part of your due diligence, the details and the way they presented will tell you a lot about the franchisor and the systems that they have developed. Manuals may look good, but ask how they are used and ask other franchisees about them if there are franchisee in the network already. The training and support documentation needs to be comprehensive; after all, that's the reason, you are thinking about joining a franchise.

So, the short answer to the question 'Does size matter?' is 'Hell no'. It's what you do with it that counts!

CHAPTER 7

THE BUSINESS MODEL

How you make your money

What Is a Business Model?

At its core, your business model is a description of how your business makes money. It's an explanation of how you deliver value to your customers at an appropriate cost.

In their simplest forms, business models can be broken into three parts:

1. **COGs**: Everything it takes to make something: design, raw materials, manufacturing, labour and so on.
2. **Cost of Sales**: Everything it takes to sell that product: marketing, distribution, delivering a service and processing the sale.
3. **Pricing and Payment**: Everything to do with how and what the customer pays: pricing strategy, payment methods, payment timing and so on.

Franchise Business Model

In a franchise business model, the franchisor is allowing the franchisee the blueprint for starting and running a proven business model. The franchisee is provided access to a national brand and support services that help the new franchise owner get up and running. In effect, the franchisor is granting access to a successful business model that they've developed.

Understanding the problem you are solving for your customers is undoubtedly the biggest challenge you'll face when you're starting a business. Customers need to want what you are selling, and your product needs to solve a real problem. But ensuring that your product fits the needs of the market is only one part of starting a successful business, and for the most part, the franchisor has developed this. The other key ingredient is figuring out how you're going to make money. This is where the business model comes into play.

There are several questions that you need to ask yourself and evaluate the franchise you are considering. These are important questions to ask the franchisor, and the franchisor needs to be able to confidently answer these questions.

- What is the problem that the business or product solves?
- Is there a market for those goods and services?
- Who are the competitors in your market?
- What are their strengths and weaknesses?
- Does the product or sector have a life cycle, and what stage is it up to?

A business model needs to include a description of a company's way of doing business; you should ask the franchisor about the aspects listed below.

Products

- You need to understand what the products are and what is the demand for those products in the market. Is the product a staple, on trend or an emerging category?
- You want a business that is differentiated from other similar players in the market.

Target customers

- Who are the customers, and can the franchisor articulate them by age, sex, demographic?
- Do they have a niche that they primarily speak to?

Value proposition

- What is the value that the product or service provides?
- How is it differentiated from the competitors in the same sector?

Distribution channels

- How are the products and services delivered: in person, bricks-and-mortar fixed location?
- Is there an opportunity for pop-up locations?
- Are sales done online?
- What third-party platforms assist with distribution?

Core capabilities

- What is the brand's product or service superpower?
- Why is the franchisor better at delivering those products or services than other franchisors or independent operators?

Commercial network

- What are the supply chain and benefits that you receive as a franchisee by being part of this network (discount process, rebates, incentives)?
- Does the franchisor have any national accounts, and do they distribute leads to the franchisee?

Partnership model

- Does the business have partnership and supply arrangements that are financially beneficial?
- Does the franchisor offer partnership options with the franchisor, or do they allow you to have a business partner in the franchise operation? If so, what are the requirements of the partners?

Cost structure

- You need to thoroughly understand the cost of every raw ingredient that goes into the make-up of the finished product and what is the recommended retail price for the products or services. Do you have flexibility with pricing and discounting?

Revenue model

- Where do the sales come from?
- What is the opportunity to upsell and cross-sell products that complement the original purchase?
- Does the franchisor know what the customer acquisition cost is? So, if you invest in marketing, what is the expected return on your investment? Most franchisors should be able to provide case studies of activities and investments and how they work.

The Business Model Canvas

The Business Model Canvas was proposed by Alexander Osterwalder based on his early book *Business Model Ontology*. It outlines nine segments, which form the building blocks for the business model in a nice one-page canvas. You can find a detailed explanation in his bestselling book, *Business Model Generation*.

The Business Model Canvas reflects systematically on your business model, so you can focus on the creation of your business model segment by segment.

This also means you can start by brainstorming and filling out the segments that spring to your mind first and then work on the empty segments to close the gaps. The following list of questions will help you brainstorm and compare several variations and ideas for your next business model innovation.

For each of the nine sections of the business model canvas, there are a number of questions to assist you in completing each segment of the canvas. These are just examples to get your juices flowing.

For those of you that have a well-established business, you might be thinking, 'I already have a business model in place'. That may well be the case, but every business needs to evolve their business model, so this exercise and the questions are worth visiting each year as part of your strategic planning activities.

You may recall in chapter 1, I introduced the idea of the internal franchisee and the external franchisee. So, if you're thinking of scaling the business, changing the business model and potentially involving other stakeholders in the business, then this process is essential.

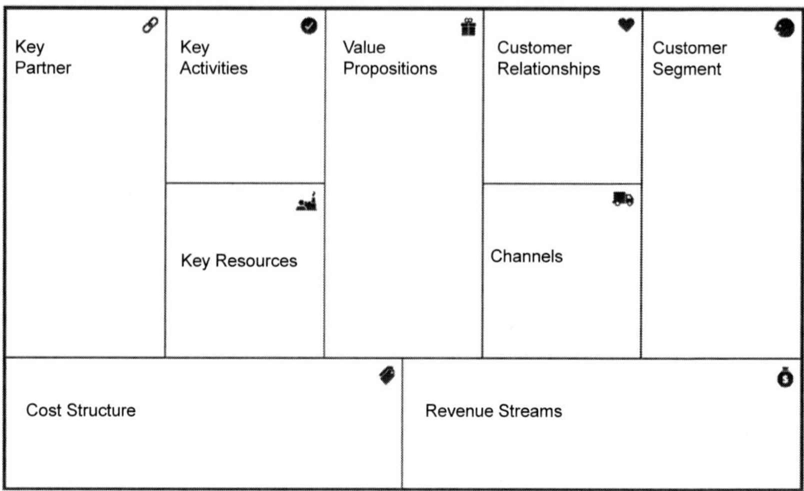

Figure 1. Business Model Canvas

Although the franchisor will provide the answers to the key elements of their business model as highlighted above. If you move forward with a business then you should complete the Business Model Canvas for your own business, answering the questions below:

Key Partners

- Who are your key partners/suppliers?
- What are the motivations for the partnerships?

Key Activities

- What key activities does your value proposition require?
- What activities are the most important in distribution channels, customer relationships and revenue stream?

Value Proposition

- What core value do you deliver to the customer?
- Which customer needs are you satisfying?

Customer Relationships

- What relationship does the target customer expect you to establish?
- How can you integrate that into your business in terms of cost and format?

Customer Segment

- Which classes are you creating values for?
- Who is your most important customer?

Key Resource

- What key resources does your value proposition require?
- What resources are the most important in distribution channels, customer relationships and revenue streams?

Distribution Channel

- Through which channels do your customers want to be reached?
- Which channels work best? How much do they cost? How can they be integrated into your and your customers' routines?

Cost Structure

- What are the biggest costs in your business?
- Which key resources/activities are the most expensive?

Revenue Stream

- What are your customers willing to pay?
- What and how do they pay recently? How would they prefer to pay?
- How much does every revenue stream contribute to the overall revenues?

Once you have completed your plans for the business model, you need to know what options are available to you, the business owner, as your way to move forward.

Airbnb

As an example, let's look at Airbnb's business model using the Business Model Canvas. Airbnb is an online marketplace that enables people to list, find and rent accommodations (single rooms, apartments, houses) for a processing fee.

Unique selling proposition

The biggest accommodation provider in the world does not own a single room. Airbnb does not rent the accommodation from the host but conveys only between supply and demand. Their business model builds on the sharing economy and on the strong belief that homeowners are willing to rent out free space to strangers.

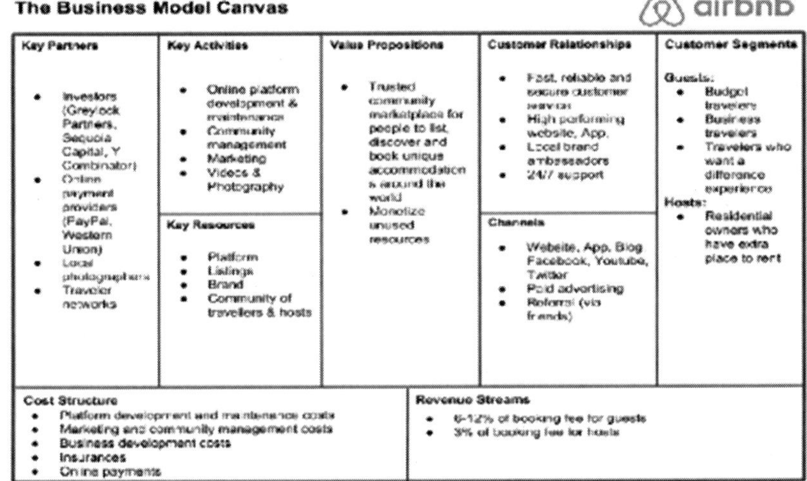

Figure 2. Airbnb's Business Model Canvas

Chick-fil-A: Business model and values

I'd like to share with you a business that I admire called Chick-fil-A. Other than being driven by their values, their business model is quite unique because Chick-fil-A retains ownership of each franchised restaurant.

Chick-fil-A selects the restaurant location and builds it, and they have a unique franchise model where a franchisee only needs to pay a $10,000 initial investment to become an operator. Each operator is handpicked and goes through a rigorous training program. The interviews plus training can take months, and it's not an easy process. Chick-fil-A states on their franchising website:

'This is not the right opportunity for you if you:

- Are seeking a passive investment in a business.
- Want to sell property to Chick-fil-A, Inc.

- Are requesting that Chick-fil-A, Inc. build at a specified location.
- Are seeking multi-unit franchise opportunities'.

They are in huge demand because the business model works, and they are super selective when choosing their business partners. For a $10,000 initial investment, the franchisee typically earns around $100,000. This is double the average wage earner and double the profit of the average small business owner in the USA. Their average store sales exceed every other QSR business in America, and here's the astonishing thing: they only trade six days a week because of their belief that Sunday is a day for rest and spending time with family — this is at the core of their values set.

They are selective in who they allow to join the business, from team members through to franchisees. It's not uncommon to have more than ten interviews, and they often tell applicants, 'If you don't intend to be here for life, you needn't apply'.

Chick-Fil-A's business model works; it requires low investment and offers a true partnership between the franchisor and franchisee, higher sales than every other QSR and excellent profitability; customers love the values, the product and the service. Their model won't suit everyone, but it works for people that share the same values. And with less than 5% operator turnover and team member turnover 50% less than other fast-food restaurants, their model is working.

If you're considering a franchise, make sure the franchisor's values are aligned with yours — this is just as important as the business model.

CHAPTER 8

WHAT IS THE BRAND?

What do you need to look for, and what are customers looking for?

Who Is the Customer?

Peter Drucker famously wrote in *The Practice of Management* that the purpose of a business is to create and keep a customer, and while I agree with elements of this, I believe it goes further than that. I believe the purpose of business is to: **Find, keep and grow the right customer.**

The 'find' is where the marketing comes in, and the 'keep' and 'grow' is where the sales process comes in, but by far the most important aspect of the marketing and sales process is ensuring that you have the 'right customer'. And this is a combination of both marketing to them and sales, selling to them.

This topic is often referred to as 'sales and marketing', but I believe you must put the activities in the right order, and marketing comes before sales. They are often intertwined or considered the same thing, but there is a clear distinction between the two.

The goal of marketing is to generate interest in a product or services and, for that marketing, to generate leads or prospects. Marketing activities include:

- Consumer research to identify the needs of the customers
- Product development — designing innovative products to meet existing or future needs
- Advertising the products to raise awareness and build the brand
- Pricing products and services to maximise long-term revenue.

On the other hand, sales activities are focused on converting prospects to actual paying customers. Sales involve directly interacting with the prospects to persuade them to purchase the product.

Marketing thus tends to focus on the broader population (or, in any case, a large set of people), whereas sales tend to focus on individuals or a small group of prospects.

I love that saying by Henry Ford:

"Half the money I spend on advertising is waste, and the problem is I do not know which half."

While there is no guarantee that all your marketing activity will work, there are ways to ensure it is more effective by talking to the right people about the right things. The way to do this is to clearly define who your ideal customer is or who the modern-day marketers refer to as your 'avatar' or 'buyer persona'.

So, let's explore how to define the right customer. To do this, there are a number of questions that you need to ask yourself:

- What is the gender, age and education of your target customer?

- What is their job?
- What is a day in their life like?
- What are their primary pain points?
- What do they value most, and what are their goals?
- Where do they go for information?
- What is important to them in selecting a provider of your product or service?
- What are the most common objections?

I'd like to provide you with three examples as references to compare with. The first is with my business, Franchise Ready. The next two are with two of brands we helped to develop, Milky Lane and Karen's Diner. Two of these businesses have clearly defined who their ideal customer is, what their problem is and how they solve that problem, whilst one of them has just gone into liquidation. All three have developed a strong brand presence and dominated in the space they chose to enter.

Milky Lane achieved a $10 million turnover in just over two years with a marketing budget of $200 per week because they knew who their customer was, what language to speak to them in and what they wanted to hear, see and experience that was different from everyone else in the same burger restaurant sector.

Karen's Diner was a phenomenon! They capitalised on a meme of a serial complainer where the name 'Karen' was given to those who complain about the most mundane issues. They had fun with it and created a restaurant chain that prided itself on delivering terrible service. Some may argue that all fast-food restaurants give terrible service, but Karen's Diner made an art form of it. They employed actors to fulfil the role of the front-of-house team, and their sole purpose was to create a theatrical experience for customers by offending them with their terrible brand of service. Theatre restaurants have been around for many years, but what the founders of Karen's Diner did so well was to capitalise on a trend and go to market very quickly. They relied on the power of social media to drive their business much like Milky Lane has done.

Karen's Diner has over 1.5 million followers on social media and over 1.5 billion views of their video posts. When they post a customer experience on social media, it goes viral, and it influences consumers to want to experience it for themselves. Their customer was someone that wanted to have a bit of fun at their friends', families' or their own expense.

I am sharing this example to illustrate the power of social media and building a brand but what it illustrates is that the hype needs to be backed up by solid operations and a product and service that has longevity.

Let's look at the examples of two brands that have done this well.

Customer Profile Franchise Ready

I started this consulting business in 2011 to assist business owners in documenting their systems to enable them to grow through franchising. Today, we are the biggest and best franchise consulting firm in Australia, with close to 50% market share in the development of franchise brands, whilst the other 40 franchise consulting firms in Australia battle out the balance of new franchise development. In 2021, Franchise Ready got recognised as the Best Franchise Consulting Business in the World as judged by Global Franchise Business magazine and the International Franchise Association.

So, let's look at how we defined our right customer.

What is the gender, age and education of your target customer?

Both male and female business owners aged 25–60. The split of business ownership in Australia is heavily skewed to males at 69%. We see many entrepreneurs without a formal university education. As much as 50% of the clients we work with are millennials, gen Y and X, with many of them going straight into business without further education.

What is their job?

Private business owners that have started a business in an industry sector and have perfected the business to the stage where customers are asking them if they are a franchise. This usually means the customers believe in the product or service and that it is delivered consistently well. Many of these business owners are technicians, excellent at the technical aspect of what they do (for instance, bakers that can bake, baristas that make great coffee, landscapers that love the outdoors and being in nature).

What is a day in their life like?

Think about what an average day is like for them, who they deal with and what affects their decision-making.

A workday for these aspiring franchise business owners has changed as they have perfected their business model. For the first few years, they may have been very hands-on but have gotten their business to a point where it doesn't require them to be 'on the tools' anymore. Often, they have opened more locations and developed new skills. They need to juggle multiple tasks, including running the business as an operator but also trying to scale their business.

Franchise Ready customers know they need to have a strategic plan but don't have the time or knowledge to get started. They are time poor and want to spend more time on the growth of the business versus the day-to-day tasks. They know that they need to document their processes and systems but never get around to it because the day-to-day operations get in the way and documenting is not their core skill.

They want to be able to get enjoyment from owning and running their own business, but they want to scale and grow but just don't know how to do it, so they spend a lot of time worrying about what's holding them back.

What are their primary pain points?

Try and describe the primary challenges they are trying to overcome that relate to your product or service.

We have identified six key challenges that these aspiring franchisors face:

- They're working in the business, not on it.
- They're making money but they're doing the majority of the work themselves.
- They don't have the capital to grow the network themselves.
- They like the idea of franchising, scaling and growing but just don't know where to start or how to use franchising to grow.
- They know that they need documented processes and systems to help scale and grow but they don't have the skillset or time to do this. It's not their core skill.
- Some aspiring franchisors may have concerns over the perception of franchising and how it is perceived partly due to some negative publicity.

Ultimately, the business owner wants more. This could be more sites, more sales, more profit, more time away from the business (whatever their more is).

What do they value most, and what are their goals?

Try and explain what they value most when making a purchasing decision (price, service, support etc.) and what they are trying to accomplish.

Franchise Ready customers know how to run their business, but they want to adapt the business so that it's less dependent on them by developing systems and processes that will enable them to grow their brand.

They want to develop a culture within the business that drives their personal vision and provides a better work–life balance.

They need a strategic plan that is manageable and dynamic.

They want to recruit people who will impact the business positively through increased productivity and profitability.

Ultimately, they want a bigger and better business.

Where do they go for information?

Think about where they go to find information to make a purchasing decision (word of mouth, friends, Google etc.).

They use the following platforms: Google, Facebook, LinkedIn and other social media, referrals from other business owners, their accountant, lawyer, family and friends and from professional associations, for those that know about the franchise associations that support franchisors and franchisees.

What is important to them in selecting a provider of your product or service?

Think about what is important when deciding between you and a competitor.

Franchise Ready customers want a trusted advisor who will mentor them based on their experience either in their own businesses or through the businesses that they have developed and supported to grow.

They want to be able to network and discuss their business challenges and successes with like-minded individuals and franchisors.

They want to take their business to the next level and increase their productivity and profitability.

They want to attract and retain talented staff and individuals with a proprietorial interest in business.

They want to develop a vision that creates a culture that delivers success.

They want to implement a strategic plan that is manageable, dynamic and delivers results.

They want to make their business less dependent on them on a day-to-day basis.

They need to learn new skills because being a franchisor requires a different set of skills applied to the core business that the aspiring franchisor created.

What are the most common objections?

List the reasons you hear from potential customers as to why your product or service doesn't fit their needs.

Franchise Ready customers are not ready to take that step — change is scary.

They don't think they are ready.

They may have a good business and don't feel that they need help.

They may have heard from people who have not had a good experience with franchising.

The cost — they currently don't see the value; they just see the cost.

They don't have time to work on the business and step out of the day-to-day.

Milky Lane

Milky Lane was the brainchild of four young entrepreneurs from Bondi Beach who wanted to create a unique and complete experience that combines amazing food with art and great music. They provide a place where customers can enjoy world-class, extreme burgers, desserts and cocktails while listening to some hip-hop or house music and admiring the old-school street art throughout the venue.

What is the gender, age and education of your target customer?

Milky Lane appeals to a broad audience of both male and female customers, with a strong female skew of over 65%. The core target audience is aged between 18–35, but there are offerings for other age profiles, including children. They are not ideal for older clientele or families with children.

A large proportion of their customer base is well educated and often very health and fitness focused, so they understand healthy food choices.

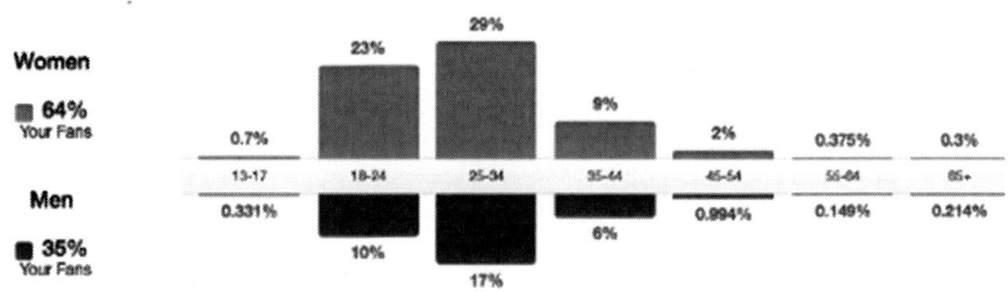

Figure 3. Milky Lane Customer Profile

What is their job?

The majority of customers are a higher demographic with high disposable income and employed in professional services, and work primarily Monday to Friday during the day.

What is a day in their life like?

They work hard in order to play hard; they enjoy eating out and experiences they can share with their friends. A significant proportion of the customers are active and attend the gym regularly.

What are their primary pain points?

They eat responsibly for the majority of the week, work hard in their jobs, and focus on their diet and fitness, so they are often looking for an outlet and a way of spoiling themselves.

What do they value most, and what are their goals?

Their customers value the relationships that they have with their friends and spending time with them. They live for now and want to celebrate life and their successes and to reward themselves for their commitment to work, health, and fitness. They want to enjoy themselves and have fun.

Where do they go for information?

Social media is the key decider in determining where they go and spend their money. Their friends and celebrities that also frequent Milky Lane venues influence the desirability and aspirational nature of visiting Milky Lane.

What is important to them in selecting a provider of your product or service?

There is a significant number of similar operators offering food and beverages, but not many of them have wrapped it all up into a destinational, aspirational, and experiential hospitality venue. Customers want somewhere special that is differentiated from competitors. They want to be seen and are happy to share that on social media for all their friends to know.

What are the most common objections?

The food is decadent and not something that you would eat every day. The restaurant is geared to a cool, young vibe and may be a little intimidating to certain audiences. For some people, the music may be a little loud. The average price is at a mid-price point, so it is not as cheap, like some other burger operators.

Milky Lane knows who their customers are and who they want them to be, and every communication they have with them is about them. Too often, marketers get caught up in being creative and espousing the features of the business, product, or service. Milky Lane knows it's about their right customer and what's important to them.

Communication with Customers

Once you have identified who your right customer is, you can then determine the best way to communicate with them and through what platforms.

There are commonly four accepted principles (Ps) of marketing, which include product, place, price and promotion. For businesses in the service industry, there are three additional Ps, which include physical environment, people and process.

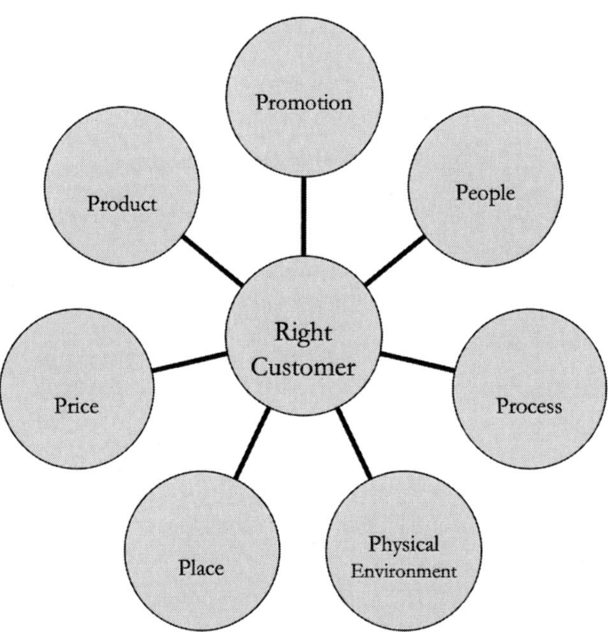

Figure 4. Principles of Marketing

We have covered a lot of detail relating to people and process so far in this book. The others need to form part of your marketing strategy and plan.

The key to any marketing plan is to ensure that it is integrated and includes a combination of marketing activities.

There are marketing gurus out there, and much material written on how to market your business. I'm not going to attempt to compete with those experts but I wanted to share with you the principles and some key takeaways that non-marketers need to know to get the right advice from marketing professionals.

I want to focus on one aspect of marketing that is fast growing and much more measurable for the marketer and the business: digital marketing. Digital marketing consists of many elements and typically deals with the marketing efforts that use an electronic device or the Internet. Businesses need to leverage digital channels, such as search engines, social media, email and their websites, to connect with current and prospective customers. As such, companies today need to have a firm grasp on how to utilise the digital universe to maximise their brand awareness and impact.

I want to share with you three examples of digital marketing from the already identified businesses referenced earlier in this chapter and another of my clients, Fitclinic: Franchise Ready representing a service-based business, and Milky Lane and Karen's Diner representing retail bricks-and-mortar businesses and Fitclinic representing a fitness brand. All of these businesses have clearly identified who the right customer is for them, and once that has been done, it is much easier to determine how you will communicate with those customers.

I have to admit when I started the Franchise Ready, I was coming from ground zero. I had just left a franchise business that didn't deliver the results that I have dreamt of. So, I was keen to get the Franchise Ready business going and get customers, and at the time, I wasn't

100% who the ideal customer was, I was happy to take anyone who would agree to use my services and pay me, and the value I put on my services was super low.

I knew about the seven Ps and that I should be following them, but I was coming from a scarcity mode, and this caused me to make some poor decisions. My price point was low, and although I followed the established process, I made concessions that affected my growth and profitability in the early stages of my business. This prevented me from marketing effectively to the right customer.

Fast forward, and my business is dramatically different. It's profitable, and the marketing activities that were generated in the first few years of operation are generating new business for me every day, often at no cost.

Although I didn't make my fortune in my previous business, it did teach me that I needed to have a balanced approach to the marketing of my business in that business. It was called IMAP, which stands for Integrated Marketing Acquisition Program. This program consisted of 27 activities that we could undertake to market that business's opportunity.

I wanted to share with you the primary activity that I undertook that generated in excess of $300,000 in sales in the past twelve months, at a minimal cost of $1,200, plus my investment in time to generate the leads the activity generated for me. That activity is perfectly designed for professional services sector or any business that is B2B, although it does have application for some B2C operators.

The activity that has generated this success for me is LinkedIn. I can remember back in the early 2000s when I first started receiving LinkedIn connection requests. I quickly dismissed it and thought it wouldn't take off. Well, I was wrong. It has single-handedly been the best marketing platform for my business. For most of my professional service and B2B clients, it has been the best of all the marketing activities that we have undertaken, and it's cheap to boot.

I'm still staggered that after starting in 2002, businesspeople have not embraced this platform. I think there is some confusion about what it is and how to use it as a marketing platform.

I'm not sure that I agree with some people's assertions that it is a form of social networking but for professionals. I believe that it is a network of some social interactions, but it's more about professional interactions and focused on professional networking rather than personal networking.

It has some elements of a social network, and there has been some change in how the platform has been used in recent times with the advent of the LinkedIn Local phenomenon, where organisers encourage people to share more about themselves personally. So, that it's not just about the person and their business profile. They are encouraging users to let people know who they are personally, as people tend to do business with people they know, like and trust. There's no better way than giving people an insight into who you are beyond the business, professional background, and resume.

I don't believe that it's a lifestyle-oriented social network in the vein of Facebook, Instagram or Google+. It's a platform for building a network of professionals with the goal of doing more business by engaging with the 'right people'.

We have used it to promote our position as thought leaders, to build a network of professionals and ultimately, to find people whom we can do business with.

Everyone should be on there but invest in getting your profile right and use it actively, as it will result in lucrative dividends.

For a business owner, the benefits are numerous, including:

- Joining relevant groups within your industry

- Education and industry commentary
- Generating leads with people that may need your products and services
- Finding key employees — if they're on LinkedIn, there's a strong chance they're open to discussion and in a lot of cases, are more professional.
- If you're thinking about franchising your business, your prospects may be listed here.
- People like to do business with people they know, like, and trust. Often, they will Google you and your company, and LinkedIn is really well optimised, making it easier to find you.

We have created a strategic approach to using LinkedIn to position ourselves within our category and to engage with our target audience that is direct, responsive and cost effective.

The second and most successful strategy we engaged in was giving people more than our competitors and more than they expected. This created us as the provider of choice and resulted in a substantial number of referrals, the cheapest form of marketing. Over 50% of our business is from referrals from satisfied clients and referral partners like lawyers and accountants. Now, some of these initiatives may not work for your business particularly if it's part of the 62% of businesses that operate in the retail sector, so let's look at a retail business that has done an amazing job building their brand.

Milky Lane

I started working with Milky Lane when they had one store operating in early 2018. Prior to the pandemic of 2020, the group grew to 16 stores with a store turnover close to $45 million. The young entrepreneurs who started the business, like most millennial and gen Y business owners, had to bootstrap their business. Their marketing budget and expenditure were just $200 per week. With a budget like that, you must really know who your customer is and ensure that you talk directly to them. The most effective way for them to do this was through a digital marketing strategy, and specifically by using the social media platforms Facebook and Instagram.

In 2018 and 2019, they were nationally recognised by The Optus My Business Awards for Best Social Media Campaign, and their marketing director Christian Avant was recognised as the Australia Social Media Influencer of The Year. At the awards evening, the owner of quite large digital marketing agency came over to our table to congratulate Christian, as he has been able to do single-handedly what significantly larger agencies have been unable to do. He commented to me, 'I don't know how he does it, but he's bloody amazing'.

To put this into perspective, let me share with you some of the incredible statistics that have been achieved through their social media strategy and activities.

On 3 November 2018, Milky Lane launched a themed cocktail beverage based on the Bubble O' Bill ice cream, and it was organically advertised on Facebook. It had a reach of:

- 693,226 unique views (unique people who saw the post)
- 143,738 engagements (how many likes and comments were received, including likes/comments on the 2,399 shares)
- 12,000 likes and 23,000 comments on the original post.

In late 2018, they had their content shared by some of the world's biggest viral pages with 2.2 million views on LadBible, 2.2 million views on FoodBible and 2.3 million views on Business Insider.

In the first week of January 2019, they had 351,950 Instagram accounts reached with 1.5 million impressions. They have had greater reach and engagement than any other food business in Australia, including McDonald's.

Quite simply, their business has been built on social media.

I am a strong believer that marketers need to be authentic. Customers are way too smart these days, and you'll be found out if you're not. Christian is truly authentic; he's not everyone's cup of tea, but what he does on social media is unparalleled. Not only is he authentic, but he's also very generous and in this section, he shares his tips for building a successful, engaging Facebook and Instagram business account and how to achieve significant organic reach that others can only ever dream of.

Facebook is constantly changing its algorithms, but as I write this section of the book, the last post Christian made this week on Facebook has over 1,200 comments without any expenditure — this result is totally organic. To put this in perspective, have a look at what your business's last post on social media achieved or better still, think of the biggest brands you can think of and see what their organic comments are. I can guarantee that won't be anything like Milky Lane.

I haven't censored his language and vernacular; as I said earlier, it's all about being authentic, and this is how Christian would tell you if he was sitting with you right now. It's possible to achieve similar results if you follow Christian's tips:

I. Know your primary target audience and deliver content that they'd want to see. Over time, it may end up being different to your original business plan but they're always #1. DON'T just continuously post what you want, post what THEY want.

II. Invest time, money and research into creating the BEST CONTENT possible. A few pics on your iPhone with shitty lighting don't cut it anymore — find someone who specialises in your field/industry and the style of content you want and plan the shoots meticulously so that you have an album full of killer material for that week or month.

III. Engage and chat with your followers. Every single person who leaves a comment on your posts is a chance to increase your reach, brand awareness and online perception etc. Listen to them and what they're saying, it's the best way to see what they really want. Ignoring them is basically saying, 'I don't give a shit' and 'I know best'.

IV. Be consistent. One good post and then 10 crap ones won't help you reach a greater audience in the long run. It takes a long while to build up an account that can achieve a large organic reach, most of which is done through consistently creating incredible content.

V. Give your brand a personality. Talk to your followers in a language they understand and BE REAL. 'Hello and thank you for your message. Pls email XYZ and someone will be in touch' is SO ROBOTIC and displeasing. Don't be afraid to have a laugh, be cheeky and ALWAYS BANTER. If there's a phrase that's red hot on the Internet right now, use that in your captions etc.

VI. Be current and on top of viral and or local trends. Sitting on what worked last year or even last month is a disaster waiting to happen. The core will always be the same, but there're constant changes or new things happening that you'll need to adapt to in order to be at the front.

VII. Engage influencers to work with and support your brand. Whether it's a paid job (which we've never done yet), or a contra deal for food/drinks/clothing etc., the power of these people on social media is VERY real. Look at the cost of the product to you that you're giving away, which is often quite small, and the potential return on that investment by generating even 10 new fans. A lot of companies say, 'Why the hell should I give them something for free? That doesn't help pay my bills'. If that's your mentality, you're in 2010 still and may as well retire.

Christian sums up, 'Some of you will skim this and think, "What does he know?", and that's totally fine. I'm not a specialist with any supersized degrees etc., ha ha ha. But there are also a lot of people who ask how we manage to achieve thousands of organic comments on Facebook or 1.5 million impressions a week on Instagram'.

The beauty of digital marketing and social media is the responsiveness and timeliness of anything that is posted. Your audience sees it and comments on it instantaneously. Social media is the modern-day secret shopper providing you feedback on your messaging and also your execution on your brand promise. So, if you get it wrong, you'll know about it, and so will everyone else.

One thing that Christian does is make comment on posts written by everyone that engages with Milky Lane on social media. It amuses me if I like, comment or share on their page, Christian engages and responds, so I always feel like they're listening.

Karen's Diner

Karen's Diner did an amazing job building a brand through social media and capitalising on a trend and this catapulted their business into the stratosphere with regards to attraction and interest, their restaurants were generating significantly higher revenue than all their comparable restaurant competitors and with over 1.5 million followers on social media and video views of over 2 billion, it's no wonder.

This phenomenal digital marketing created a desire in the minds of consumers to experience the 'terrible service' they had to offer. I opened this chapter mentioning the importance of Marketing and Sales, Karen's Diner did an amazing job with their marketing and getting the brand into the consideration set of consumers, unfortunately the brand didn't have longevity, for a few reasons, The speed to market meant they didn't have solid operational foundations and for many customers, whilst they may have enjoyed the entertainment aspect of their restaurant visit, the food was not good enough to warrant repeat visitation. This is where the sales component of 'Marketing & Sales' kicks in, the marketing gets them in the door, but the experience keeps them coming back and sadly this caused the demise of this meteoric restaurant chain.

So, the lesson here, is to be strong and relevant with your marketing but make sure your execution is first rate as that will determine the ongoing success of a business.

Fitclinic

I have been working with the founder, Aaron King for a while and he has created an amazing business, one that I have been using for over 6 years, they are the best at what they do, the problem is a large percentage of the population don't know what an exercise physiologist is, what they do and why they are different from other fitness options.

Aaron has been building a profile on social media for Fitclinic amongst other initiatives to build profile and to educate the marketplace, but it had been a slow burn because his messaging was like everyone else in the fitness space (with the exception of those brands that have glamour models posing in their photos, as Aaron is no glamour model!). Recently Aaron changed his approach and identified how he could position his brand differently from what is a very crowded marketplace. When he and his team do video shoots and education pieces to camera for social media, they often have a blooper reel, so they started posting it and the digital audience engaged with those posts and then Aaron realised he was on to something and that people were sick of seeing the stereotypical fitness posts with beautiful people doing perfect exercises and in so doing making the majority of us develop an inferiority complex.

Aaron has identified that humour works and being able to relate to people and how the majority of the population feel about fitness and exercise. His posts on social media have increased by thousands of percent and some of his posts have made millions of impressions and he's become an Instagram celebrity when he walks down the street, the irony of this is he used to laugh at others that focussed on building their social profile but what he has demonstrated is that if talk to your audience the way they want to receive and digest the information (and adding humour) goes a log way to getting engagement and driving the business.

The initiatives that he has taken in communicating to an audience in a way that resonates with them has done amazing things for the profile of the business and the positive results that it is having on membership and franchise enquiry levels.

With a clear digital and social media strategy your business will thrive. I often get asked how much a business should be spending on marketing, and that's a really difficult question to answer without knowing the answers to the following questions:

- What is the objective of your marketing activity? Is it to generate leads or to build the brand?
- What marketing activities have you done previously?
- Do you or have measured the financial returns of other marketing initiatives?
- What do you consider a fair return on your investment? (It is commonly accepted that a $4 return for each dollar spent is desirable.)
- Do you have a budget?

If you are able to answer those questions, the marketing can be more targeted.

My recommendation for business owners based on my experience is that they should never stop marketing, as it is the continuity of activity that reinforces the brand in the consumer's mind. And when they need your products or services, they will only remember you if you're communicating your products, services and brand.

"The man who stops advertising to save money is like the man who stops the clock to save time."

—Thomas Jefferson, third American president

New businesses need to spend at least 10% of their revenue initially, and then, this could settle at 5% of revenue. Franchise businesses typically collect between 2% to 3.5% of revenue, which goes into a marketing fund to be used for the benefit of the whole brand and network. One of the key attributes of a franchise business is the brand awareness that the franchisor has generated. This enables them to spend a lower percentage of turnover on marketing because of the longevity of the marketing activity and the buying power of having a bigger marketing budget.

We conducted some research with business owners and asked them what they would do differently if they had their time over again, knowing what they know now back when they started their businesses. 38% of them said they would have spent more time marketing, and 35% of them said they wished they had spent more money marketing their business when they started it.

All this discussion on marketing is about 'finding the right customer' and generating interest in your products and services, and hopefully generating prospects and leads that will try your business. This is where the second part of the marketing and sales equation comes into play — sales.

Sales is what happens at the coalface, that moment of truth when the prospect tries your business and becomes a customer. A customer comes once but what every business needs is repeat business; we need customers to come back again and again and become clients.

Everything you do at an operational level will influence the 'keeping and growing the right customer', and that is why the processes and systems we discussed in chapter 7 are so important. Every business needs operational standards and a process for delivering service excellence.

Ray Kroc explained in his autobiography how he learned an important lesson:

"You could influence people with a smile and enthusiasm and sell them a sundae when what they'd come in for was a cup of coffee."

—Ray Kroc

The key point I'd like to make in closing out this chapter is that what I have shared with you in this chapter relates to the franchisor and what they need to be doing to invest in the brand, so you need to be asking them how they have and will continue to build the brand.

Whilst most franchisors have a responsibility to build the brand and many have marketing co-operative funds to facilitate this, your role as the franchisee is to invest in your business, in your local area marketing and in the experience that you deliver to your customers. You need to become part of your local community, you need to own it, give back and invest in local area marketing.

Although you may be limited with what you can do with social media and the brand, you can build your own brand through the excellence that you deliver to your customers in every experience that they have with you and your business. Business success is all about positioning and execution.

I trademarked The Franchise Guy as that is how I positioned myself in the franchising sector. I've built a personal brand, and you can do the same through how you operate your business and present yourself to your community regardless of what business you are in.

CHAPTER 9

RETURN ON CAPITAL INVESTMENT

Show Me the Money

Poor financial management led to the closure of one of my first clients as a business coach. It devastated me, and I felt like I should have done more. I should have known something was wrong when he wouldn't provide me with his P&Ls and balance sheet, and then when he sent me a cheque in the mail for his coaching fees, I realised something wasn't right as all his other payments were direct debit.

This was a family-operated business that had been operating for over 50 years, with three generations of family members working in the business and 25 staff members, all with families. This was a bad situation for everyone that could have been avoided with better financial management.

It was a salient moment for me, and it made me more vigilant in addressing the financial management of a business with all the clients that I work with.

Setting up to be a successful business is no easy feat. It requires guts, hard work and a good system, particularly when it comes to financial management. Running a successful business means that you now have even more responsibilities on your shoulders than you ever did as an employee. Your employees are dependent on you, and any decision that you take will affect not only you but your team as well. Good leaders should always evaluate every decision they make with thought and caution, particularly when it involves handling business finances.

I want to start by talking about capital, and specifically, the capital required to go into business. I can speak with experience about being undercapitalised myself. In several franchise businesses that I worked in, franchisees were undercapitalised. It can have an impact on the business, and the mental and financial state of the business owners concerned.

Every business needs the capital to get started. The problem entrepreneurs and business owners, particularly the risk-takers, have is that they are optimistic and only see the best possible scenarios. They can often go into business undercapitalised by underestimating the true costs of operating while overestimating the sales their business may generate.

Financial Model

The starting point for any business is the creation of a financial model and financial plan, and we referred to this as the business model in chapter 7. The business model can be broken into three parts to determine the financial requirements and decisions that need to be made:

- **COGs:** everything it takes to make something: design, raw materials, manufacturing, labour, and so on.

- **Cost of sales:** everything it takes to sell that product: marketing, distribution, delivering a service, and processing the sale.
- **Pricing and payment:** everything pertaining to how and what the customer pays: pricing strategy, payment methods, payment timing and so on.

The franchisor should have perfected the business model and be able to explain the three elements of their business model. Many franchisors will have created a financial modelling tool to assist you with your evaluation of the business opportunity. The Franchise Disclosure Document (FDD) will outline the key costs, and some franchisors (all of them in the USA) provide a statement that shows what the lower, middle and upper quartile of franchisee performance is in their network, so that you can see best and worst-case scenarios. If the franchisor doesn't provide this information, you should ask them for it.

The financial modelling tool is designed to show you what your investment level, expected return on capital and profitability will be, based on different revenue and cost control assumptions that can be provided by existing franchisees or through the company-operated units of the franchisor.

If your franchisor has not developed a financial model, it is well worth you completing your own version to properly evaluate the opportunity and engaging a professional to assist.

Here is an example of one of the clients that we have worked with; this is their franchise financial model.

Franchisee Financial Model

Important notice

The sheet calculates the project returns based on your inputs and assumption on the "inputs" sheet
Fat Jak's takes no responsibility for the data you enter into this spreadsheet or the forward projections and earnings. Please seek accounting

Payback period and returns (Average Store)

	Year 0	Year 1	Year 2	Year 3	Year 4	Year 5
Establishment Costs	351,000					
Revenue		1,710,000	1,890,000	1,984,500	2,083,725	2,187,911
Cost of Goods Sold		547,200	604,800	635,040	666,792	700,132
Gross Profit		1,162,800	1,285,200	1,349,460	1,416,933	1,487,780
Expenses						
Royalty		85,500	94,500	99,225	104,186	109,396
Marketing Levy		34,200	37,800	39,690	41,675	43,758
Franchisee salary		60,000	60,360	60,722	61,086	61,453
Other Staff Salaries		550,000	553,300	556,620	559,960	563,319
Other expenses		296,810	307,734	316,850	326,336	336,210
Total Expenses		1,026,510	1,053,694	1,073,107	1,093,243	1,114,136
EBITDA		136,290	231,506	276,353	323,690	373,644
Add back franchisee salary		60,000	60,360	60,722	61,086	61,453
Franchise Net Benefit	-351,000	**196,290**	**291,866**	**337,075**	**384,776**	**435,097**
Cumulative net benefit	-351,000	-154,710	**137,156**	**474,231**	**859,007**	**1,294,104**
Payback Period (in years)		1.53				

Figure 5. Franchisee Finance Model

In this model, you can see the initial investment and a summary of revenue and expenses and profitability (EBITDA) and ultimately, the return on capital.

It's critically important that you understand the KPIs of the business you are considering, what are the industry benchmarks and how is the business that you are considering measuring up?

Break-even Point

To be profitable in business, it is important to know what your break-even point is. Your break-even point is the point at which total revenue equals total costs or expenses. At this point, there is no profit or loss — in other words, you break even.

The formula is:

$$\textit{Break-even point} = \frac{\textit{Fixed costs}}{\begin{gathered}\textit{Total sales revenue} - \textit{Cost to make product}\\ \textit{(Contribution margin)}\end{gathered}}$$

To better explain what all of this means, let's look at a breakdown of the formula components.

Fixed costs

Fixed costs are not affected by the number of items sold. Fixed costs are required to be paid regardless of the sales generated. Examples include rent, fixed wages and salaries, lease costs and loan repayments, contracts entered into and legal and accounting costs. Fixed costs also include fees paid for services like graphic design, advertising and PR.

Variable costs

Variable costs are those that vary with sales, such as wages, utilities and COGs and materials used in the production of the finished product that is sold to customers.

Contribution margin

The contribution margin is calculated by subtracting the variable costs from the selling price. Any money left after that represents your net profit.

Contribution margin ratio

This figure is usually expressed as a percentage. It's calculated by subtracting your fixed costs from your contribution margin.

Profit earned following your break-even

Once your sales amount equals your fixed and variable costs, you have reached the break-even point. To illustrate this exercise, let me share with you the break-even for one of my clients. They are a food franchise business.

Their weekly fixed costs are:

Rent	$1,300
Wages	$3,200
Loan repayments	$1,000
Marketing	$ 500
Accounting	$ 200
Total fixed costs	**$6,200**

Their weekly variable costs are:

Food and packaging	$4,000
Casual wages	$ 500
Utilities	$ 300
Office expenses	$ 200
Operating supplies	$ 200
Miscellaneous costs	$ 400
Total variable costs	**$5,600**

Sales ($20,000)-Costs ($5,600)=Contribution margin ($14,400)

Contribution margin = 57%

Break-even point = $11,800 per week in sales

The business starts to make profit on every dollar over the break-even sales of $11,800. Once a business owner knows their break-even sales, they can focus on sales-building activities and control costs accordingly.

When starting a business and completing a break-even analysis, much of it is based on assumptions and projections unless you are part of an established business model like a franchise system. This is one of the many benefits associated with franchising: the fact that it is a proven model perfected over time and should provide the business owner with a more accurate estimate of income and expenses.

Either way, the break-even analysis should be completed regularly, as should the contribution margin, as this will help you analyse the profitability of products and assist in determining the ideal price or continued viability of a product.

In rough terms, the contribution margin ratio will give an indication of the likely percentage of additional revenue that drops to the bottom line as profit. Knowing this can be quite motivating and assist the business owner in making good decisions.

If you need to get money from a finance company, you will need to complete a business plan which includes the business model and the break-even analysis. The creation of a budget and cash flow forecast is essential for financiers to consider your application. But even more important is factoring any borrowings into your forecasts and knowing that you have the ability to service the debt, and what the finance does to your break-even and profitability.

My Mistakes

When I started all my businesses, I did all the bookkeeping and accounting work myself. Not content with working fulltime and between six and seven days a week, I would do my bookkeeping on the lounge in front of the television at night. I would drive my wife mad.

Many business owners start doing their own books, and there are definite benefits to doing this, as it enables you to manage the cash coming in and going out (cashflow) and gives you a good handle on the business. Some of us think we are saving money by doing it ourselves, but it's a bit of a false economy because often we're not good at it, and we resent it and what it does to our free time. Often, it takes us much longer to do it than a professional would take, and sometimes we get it wrong. Thankfully, there are some fantastic accounting software systems available now that make it much easier to manage your books.

Sound bookkeeping is the basis for all financial management.

It is important to set things up correctly from the start and get the professional advice that you need. I must admit to doing it cheaply by doing it myself and not having the right accountant to advise me when I started my franchisor business with the Alternative Board. Fast forward four years, and I had to go back and fix it, and it cost me thousands of dollars to get it right and set it up properly. So, my strong advice is to invest in the finance function early on, and as soon as you can afford to engage a good bookkeeper to do your bookkeeping work.

Get a strong financial advisor to help you set up and to advise you. I used cheap services, and here's the thing with cheap: it's just not good value. In 2019, I spent double what I should have because I had to get work redone. Pay a little bit more for the right person.

KPIs

It is worth engaging a strong finance person to create all your finance set-up functions, including a chart of accounts, accounting software and set-up, budgets, cash flow forecasting, break-even analysis and to help develop your business model.

Once you're up and going, make sure that you complete monthly P&Ls and cash flow forecasts. A P&L statement is the best tool for knowing if your business is profitable, and a cash flow statement will help you know what's coming and what to plan for.

Each month, you should analyse your P&L and create an action plan to improve areas of opportunity. But don't wait till the end of the month, as by then it will be too late. You need to establish KPIs that you measure every day and those that you measure every week so that you can adjust course if need be.

"You can't manage what you can't measure."
—Peter Drucker

When I was at McDonald's, we measured everything. Sometimes, we measured the ridiculous: we used to determine our yields, which meant how many finished servings we received for a raw ingredient. A good example of why I say it was ridiculous was because we measured our French fries yield (how many servings of fries per 100 kg of raw product) by counting the number of fry bags and boxes. The reason this was crazy was because of waste and the sheer number of fry bags and boxes we had in store and the potential for errors. This resulted in huge variances.

A smarter way to measure was to determine how many French fries went into a serving by dividing the number of servings sold through the cash register system by the weight of fries used. This showed you whether you were getting the optimum number of finished goods from the raw ingredients used. The McDonald's fries yield was 840–880 small servings per 100 kg. If you got fewer servings, you may have been overfilling bags or had bad controls. If you got a higher yield, then potentially, customers weren't getting the correct-sized serving. Knowing this information enabled you to go and observe operations and see where the problem was so you could do something about it.

Product Cost

Every product at McDonald's had a yield to enable them to measure the profitability of the production processes. One of the other key measurements at McDonald's was determining the optimum cost of producing a product versus the actual cost achieved in the production of the product.

For example, a cheeseburger had a range of raw ingredients: bun, meat patty, mustard, ketchup, pickle, onion and a slice of cheese. The process to determine the food cost of making the cheeseburger was adding all the raw costs. Back when I worked there, the cost was around 40¢, and we sold the burger for $1.60, resulting in a food cost of 25%.

If all we sold was cheeseburgers, and we sold 1,000 of them, our sales would be $16,000, and our costs should have been $4,000, so our optimum cost of raw ingredients would be 25%. If the actual cost of what we bought was less, then either we had a stocktaking error or we weren't putting the right amount of ingredients on the burger (some stores had one-pickle days, which saved money — this was unsanctioned). If the actual food cost was higher than 25%, then we had an operational problem, and our control measures weren't in place. Our allowed variance was 0.3%, and stores that had good controls were able to achieve this.

The reason for describing this scenario is that every business needs to know what the optimum cost of production should be and determine what it is. If there is a variance, you need to investigate the reasons — that's good financial management.

In order to do that, you need to have a strong financial model.

Working Capital

Your budget will be your roadmap for financial success, and the KPIs and P&L reports will be your measurement. It's important to know what industry benchmarks are and how you compare. This information is easy to find online, and if you're in a franchise system industry or considering becoming a franchisee, then you will have other similar businesses to use as the benchmark.

When I worked in a very large recruitment business, we made it a requirement that our franchise owners maintained three months' working capital, and they had to provide us with a statement each month to verify this. We did this because of the nature of that industry, but also because it was just good practice. If you have three months of working capital (your break-even costs), you can confidently make investment decisions that don't compromise the cashflow of the business.

With all the business owners I work with, I instil the need to have three months' working capital, especially if they are thinking of investing in additional resources or products, as this mitigates risk.

Financial Management

I currently have two clients who have included the full financial function in their franchise business model. They do everything for the franchisee and in doing so, have the systems set up and streamlined for efficiency. This enables the franchisee to focus on the core operations without the distraction of the finance function. And for the franchisor, they know exactly where each franchisee is with cash flow and profitability and are able to react quickly if help is needed.

Good financial management is the key to the success of every business, but in a franchise system, good financial management results in a better return on investment (ROI). To give you some idea of what can be achieved, I have provided the average return on capital investments as a guide for you when considering a business opportunity and a way to measure your own success. Here is a rough guide:

- Businesses under $100,000 may take 12 to 24 months
- Businesses from $180,000 to $400,000 may take 2.5 to 3.5 years
- Businesses from $500,000 to $850,000 may take around four years
- Businesses over $1 million may take five or more years.

For those considering franchising as their way to enter business, franchisees typically spend seven years in a network which, if they are successful, allows them to realise ample goodwill value upon the sale of their business.

Good financial management enables better financial performance and a cleaner set of books. This is particularly important when it comes time to sell. I know from experience that the better the books, the better the controls and the better the profitability. This results in a better valuation and a quicker sale of the business.

Every business will sell, so preparing for it is a must. Get the right advice, set your financial plans, and controls up correctly from the start, and create financial disciplines every day, week and month. The more efficient and effective you are at the start, the easier it will be throughout and at the end.

CHAPTER 10

SUPPORT

Partnerships and Family

Partnerships can be amazing, but they can also be extremely stressful. I have been in 10 business partnerships and not all of them have been good: three of them have ended in the closure of the business, significant losses of investment capital, termination of the broader partnership agreement and in two cases irreconcilable differences with those business partners.

There are some obvious benefits to partnerships, and I have benefitted from them but have also been on the flipside when partnerships didn't go well.

There are three types of partnership to consider in franchising; the most important partner is the familial one. If you're considering buying a franchise, you must have the full support of your family. Every member of the family needs to know the impact that going into business will have on your life, your income, your time with family and the demands the business will place on you physically and psychologically. All too often, I have seen partners in life often having different behavioural profiles, desires and motivations in life, so discussing what business ownership means to the relationship is very important. Ultimately, the reality is your life will change and you and your family need to be ready for it.

Many franchisors refer to their franchisees as franchise partners. The thinking behind this is to demonstrate that the relationship you are about to enter is a partnership where both parties contribute to the business success and both parties receive a return from the business partnership. Philosophically, this is an endearing term and reflects the desire of the franchisor to partner with the franchisee. The best way to see if, in fact, the franchisor does partner with their franchisees is to conduct good validation with existing franchisees, as they will tell you what the relationship is like between the franchisor and franchisees. You should look for a franchisor that lives these values and has a demonstrable track record of supporting their franchisees.

If a franchisee wants to enter into a partnership agreement with a franchise, the franchisor will have a couple of requests. Firstly, they will ask to receive a copy of the partnership agreement so that they understand who the partners are, and they will often need to meet all partners and will certainly have to approve a change in ownership structure during the term of the franchise agreement.

The other key requirement of the franchisor will be to have a nominated manager/lead of the partnership, which is the person that the franchisor will communicate with as the franchisor will want one main point of contact and not have to deal with multiple representatives.

Traditional Partnerships

There are three types of partnership arrangements that fall under this category. In particular, in a partnership business, all partners share liabilities and profits equally, while in others, partners may have limited liability. There also is the so-called silent partner, which is the party not involved in the day-to-day operations of the business.

A partnership is a common business structure involving two or more people. Importantly, the laws applicable to a partnership differ between each state and territory. In Australia, there are three types of partnerships and similar variations in other parts of the world:

- A normal partnership
- A limited partnership
- An incorporated limited partnership.

Normal Partnership

A normal partnership is the most common and only type of partnership that does not require registration. It is appropriate for multiple people looking to run a business together using a simple structure.

It does not require a written agreement to be formed. Rather, determining whether a normal partnership exists will depend on various factors, such as whether partners share business profits and whether the property is owned by partners together.

Although it is not a legal requirement to have a written agreement, it is my strong recommendation that there be a documented partnership agreement, which outlines the key terms, roles and responsibilities and standard partnership/shareholders agreement terms.

Each partner is jointly responsible for the business's obligations, such as its debts. In terms of tax obligations, the partnership needs to lodge a tax return annually, and each partner must pay tax on their respective share of income for that year.

Limited Partnership

A limited partnership is one of two types that need to be registered. Although not required, it is beneficial to create a written partnership agreement.

The point of difference with a limited partnership is that there must be at least:

- One general partner who plays an active role in the management of the partnership. However, general partner(s) are also responsible for all of the debts of the partnership.
- One limited partner who plays a passive role in the management of the partnership. Limited partner(s) are also only responsible for a limited amount of the debts of the partnership.

There can only be up to 20 general partners in the partnership. However, there are no restrictions on the number of limited partners in the partnership.

In terms of tax obligations, certain limited partnerships are taxed as separate legal entities.

Incorporated Limited Partnership

An incorporated limited partnership is the other type that needs to be registered. It is set up as a company and is normally used for venture capital investment purposes. Many franchisors will not like to enter into a franchise agreement with an incorporated limited partnership, so you should check with the franchisor before incurring those costs.

Like a limited partnership, an incorporated limited partnership also involves general partner(s) and limited partner(s). There can only be up to 20 general partners in the partnership. There are also no restrictions on the number of limited partners in the partnership.

However, limited partners are not responsible for the debts of the partnership. Instead, the general partner(s) are personally responsible for any failure of the partnership to meet its obligations.

Famous Business Partnerships

Think about famous Australian business partnerships that are also life partners — Gerry Harvey and Katie Page (Harvey Norman), Cliff Obrecht and Melanie Perkins (Canva) — or American business mega stars, such as Melinda and Bill Gates. Or Jay-Z and Beyoncé. These famous business partner couples have made it look relatively easy. What you don't see, though, is the hard work they likely had to go through to create a partnership that works for both their personal and business lives. If you're considering taking your relationship into a business partnership, here are some practical considerations to help you keep both your romance and business alive and well.

Remember why you decided to go into business together in the first place. Marriage therapists often advise couples to think back to what drew them together in the first place. This is a great exercise because it helps them remember the passion and excitement of their earlier time together, in hopes that it will motivate them to work on their current relationship. The same holds true of a business partnership. Remember why you thought this was a good idea. Was it to garner more time for togetherness? Was it because the thought of working together sounded fun since you already were having a great time together? Whatever the reason, hold onto that passion and drive and revisit it often.

Designate one of you as the final decision-maker. Remember the franchisor will want you to nominate who that will be, and they will only deal with that partner for anything that relates to the franchise agreement.

Determine what each of your strengths and passions are and divide the responsibilities accordingly. Having them documented with the way you are going to measure what success looks like will ensure role clarity.

Try to resolve your differences in private and always present a unified front in front of others. People may know about your personal and business relationship, but no one will want to get in the middle of a heated discussion between you two. Nor do they want to appear to take sides, so it's your job as owners to avoid confrontations that would put someone in that most uncomfortable position.

If you and your spouse like to do the same things or have the same kind of skill set, this may be a challenge for you. There are many responsibilities in every business, and in most businesses, it starts with sales. Are one of you ready to become the salesperson/spokesperson? What about the bookkeeping and finances? Is this a skill one of you possesses, or do you need to hire it out? Long before becoming business partners, you probably knew each other's strengths. Now is the time to master them where appropriate for your business.

Stephen Covey coined the phrase 'Start with the end in mind' in his book *The 7 Habits of Highly Effective People*. You should have some very clear and specific goals in mind when starting any new venture. Ask yourself the following questions:

- Do you both want the same outcome?
- What is your exit strategy?
- How will you share the profits?
- Will you get other family members involved?
- How many hours will you work, and how will you be compensated?

Write these questions and answers to them down and continue reflecting on them on a regular basis.

Family

Hire family carefully and treat them as you would any employee. Many family businesses are truly that: businesses that employ children, parents, siblings, in-laws and friends. A lot of children and family members get to cut their teeth in business by being part of a family venture. This teaches them strong values and work ethic, but it is critical that these family members are treated the same as other employees. It is important that family does not feel entitled.

I've seen family businesses and relationships break down because of the difficulty of working with family and friends and not delineating the roles and communication required. It could be said that family members should work harder than an employee, but this may not happen if the ground rules are not set right from the beginning.

Being in business with the people you love and trust can be the wisest decision you make as you enter the franchise industry. After all, the skills that make you great romantic partners, family or friends are the very same that have the potential to make.

Some of the reasons for entering a partnership include:

- Sharing the risk
- Sharing the capital requirements to establish the business.
- Bringing in additional or complementary skills and experience
- Ability to share responsibility and have time away from the business.

It is common for franchisees to look for partners, especially in capital-intensive franchise segments. However, there are pros and cons to franchise partnerships, which need to be managed.

Things to Do Before Entering a Franchise Partnership

Take help from a lawyer to properly frame a franchise partnership agreement. It should include the following:

- Role of each partner
- Profit share
- Expenses for each partner
- Partnership dissolving terms etc.

An expert franchise lawyer will be able to provide more business-specific items that need to be included in a franchise agreement.

Advantages of Franchise Partnerships

Sharing Costs

Buying a franchise can be expensive, and if you go with a franchise partnership, then these expenses can be shared, and you needn't spend all of your savings.

Sharing Responsibilities

If you go for it alone, every responsibility, including finance, operations, marketing, sales, customer relationships etc. is on you. But, with a partner, it can be shared to tap the best of both your capabilities.

Stronger Team for Initial Promotions and Marketing

During the initial stages of running a franchise, word of mouth helps a lot in establishing the business. If you have an experienced business partner by your side, then you have a wider circle of family, friends, and business connections to help you out.

More Creativity and Problem-solving Ability

With two minds to focus on the business, expect more creativity and problem-solving skills. If you run into startup issues, then both of you can put your heads together to work towards finding a resolution.

Disadvantages of Franchise Partnerships

Just like the advantages, there are a few disadvantages to franchise partnerships, too.

Profit and Success Are Shared

When you have a partner, you must share both the profit and the reputation of the business, regardless whether both partners work for the franchise or not.

Difficulty in Making Business Decisions

Sometimes it is critical to take immediate business decisions, and if all the franchise partners are not in perfect sync, then even simple decisions may take longer than expected. A clear division of responsibilities in the franchise agreement requirement of the nominated manager and in a well-written partnership/shareholders agreement can take care of this issue to a large extent.

My Experiences with Partnerships

There are three main issues that I have seen in partnerships that create problems.

- **Contribution** — One party feels like they are contributing more to the success of the business and resent this and the distribution of salary and profit dividends based on this supposed contribution. Leave your ego at the door. Usually, you need an entrepreneurial spirit and a big dose of courage to go into business or enter into a franchise agreement, so you and your partner may have strong and determined personalities. While these traits can help you succeed in business, they can also put a strain on a franchise partnership.

  The only way for the partnership to work is for both parties to act with understanding and humility. Rather than focus on your own agenda, you and your partner should do whatever it takes to help your business develop and grow. Always keep the collective, and not the individual, in mind.
- **Communication** — Not having regular meetings to review the business performance and discomfort in bringing issues up for discussion, often letting them fester till they get to breaking point. Collaboration and trust are imperative so regular and honest communication is a must.
- **Accountability** — Not having a clear delineation of roles and responsibilities and accountability of results against those roles and responsibilities. Having the same core values is equally important. Of course, you may have differing opinions once in a while, but your shared values and key mission will help you achieve your objectives.

A couple of initiatives that I have used and that some of my clients have used that incorporate partnerships into the business management include offering a minority shareholding to key members of the team. What this does is garner greater commitment from key team members involved in the day-to-day management of the business. This can be done in a few ways:

- Give key team members an equity stake in the business at a discounted rate to the actual value. I have one client that grants up to 10% of the business and discounts this shareholding by 50% to ensure the team member sees the value.
- Give team members sweat equity, which is where you enable a key team member to acquire equity in the business over a period. This can be either gifted to them or allocated on a discounted basis.
- Enter into a partnership agreement of up to 50% of the value of the investment and provide a vendor loan for any shortfall the partner may have to put towards the capital contribution to the business. This may include an interest component.
- Although not a traditional partnership, offering profit share to key employees gives them a sense of ownership and, in my experience, has delivered a proprietary ownership and more responsibility with those team members to whom I have offered this to. They know the better the business performs, the more opportunities for additional income are available. This has enabled me to own and operate as many as six businesses at any time.

In Summary

If things are working well for everyone, then franchise partnerships are worth it. Conversely, personal or professional issues affecting your partnership will cost you and the franchise business big time. Make sure your behavioural styles and personalities complement each other. You don't have to be the same; in fact, you want and need someone that is different from you. I wrote earlier about the benefit of having different approaches and the balance between the risk-seeker and the risk-tolerator.

Ensure that there is a clear delineation of how the partnership will work, and ensure you choose a partner who is both professionally successful and a sensible person to work with. If you can't agree on these areas before you go into business together, you might end up jeopardising the success of your unit in the long run.

I have been in 10 business partnerships. I like them, but as I mentioned earlier, not all of them have worked out. But following the principles outlined in this chapter will give you a greater chance of a successful partnership and business. Those business partnerships that did not work for me didn't work because I was a minority shareholder/partner and I didn't work in those businesses, so my impact was minimal and there were majority shareholders/partners that ran the day-to-day operations of the business. My strongest piece of advice if you are considering a business partnership is to make sure that you have a majority shareholding.

CHAPTER 11

DISCOVERY

What Are They Really Like?

In order to know if the franchisor is the right person for you to partner with or join a business with, you really need to get to know them and their business intimately, and there are several ways to do this — interviewing franchisees, searching online reviews of the franchisor, reviewing how your application has been managed by the key executives in the business and the overall professionalism of the process they use to recruit franchisees. All these initiatives are important, but attending a discovery day will give you the final verification if this business may be the right business for you, and for that purpose, you should visit the franchisor's head office.

The discovery day is a face-to-face meeting, usually at the head office of the franchise company, which takes place between one or more prospective buyers and the franchise company. It's called this because it used to be the way that prospective buyers discovered who ran the company and learned about the company and ownership opportunity. Today, the Internet allows prospective buyers to research much of the information they would have learned at discovery day, but it doesn't allow prospects to have a face-to-face meeting with the executive team. This is one of the biggest benefits of discovery day. Meeting the executive team allows prospective buyers to get a true feeling for what the company is about, what their beliefs are and what they believe is the key to being successful.

During the pandemic, many discovery days and interviews took place online. Although this can expedite the process and you can see the people that you are dealing with, nothing can substitute seeing the franchisor and their support team in their offices.

The discovery day is so called because it is a day of *discovery*. For the franchisor and for you, the prospective franchisee. It's your chance to discover what it's like at the head office and who the team that are going to support you are, who they are as people and as franchise executives, what their values are, what the culture, their vison and mission for their business and their franchisees are.

Whilst you're evaluating them, they're evaluating you and determining if you're the right fit for their business. Usually, the owner, founder, CEO and key executive team will be in attendance so they can determine if you're the right fit. The best franchisors never sell a franchise, they grant the rights to the 'right' franchisee. For this reason, they need to interview you, spend time with you and understand why you are going to be the right fit for them and uphold the standards and the brand that they have created, they're putting a lot of trust in you to use and represent their brand.

You must be officially 'invited' to a discovery day. You will be invited as long as you've been doing what's been asked of you — if you've been participating in the franchisors' sales process and you're financially qualified to purchase the franchise.

When Do I Go to a Discovery Day?

Believe it or not, not everyone is invited. If you are lucky enough to be invited, that means that the franchise company believes you may be a good match with them to become a franchise owner. It is very likely that you will speak with a franchise development person at the franchise company many times on the phone before you are invited to attend a day of discovery. During the time the franchise development person is getting to know about you, you should be doing the same about the company. This will ensure that you have quality questions to ask when you are there, and you can make sure that your time spent at discovery day is worth it. It is, though, important to remember this is the franchise's most ideal time to 'put their best foot forward'. Don't let this distract you from getting important questions answered.

Most franchisors will have a rigorous recruitment process, and they should share this with the franchisee so that the franchisee knows what to expect in the recruitment process. The discovery day is usually the last step in the recruitment process before a decision is made by both parties.

The agenda of the day is normally jam-packed and may include interviewing existing franchisees or visits to existing franchisee's locations to see firsthand what the business is like. I strongly recommend that you ask the franchisor if they offer 'store days' or 'on-the-job evaluations' (OJEs). The OJE is a structured day in the business with an existing franchisee and a member of the franchisor's executive team. The objective of the OJE is to give you a hands-on experience of the business so that you can evaluate the opportunity and see if you can see yourself working in that franchise business, whilst the franchisor and franchisee (whose location you are working in) get to evaluate you and determine if they think you are the right fit for the business.

The OJE may be completed prior to the discovery day or, depending on location and franchisors' process, it may be part of the discovery day. Either way, it is extremely valuable for all parties to properly evaluate the suitability (of you and the business).

Do Not Attend a Discovery Day, If...

Don't attend a discovery day if you're on the fence about the opportunity. *Only* go to a discovery day if you're pretty much ready to say yes, you've done all or at least most of your franchise research, you've started to arrange financing (if needed) and you have a franchise lawyer in mind that you'll be using if you are offered a franchise. (Not everyone is offered the right to a franchise. But most people are if they've been invited to a discovery day.)

Finally, don't attend a discovery day if you're just curious about the business. It will be a waste of time for both parties.

Use the questions provided in chapter 13 to quiz the existing franchisees in the network and to ask about the franchisor. This list is by no means exhaustive but covers the important questions that are relevant to most franchise applicants. You may also have some questions of your own that relate to your personal situation, or you just may be more detail oriented than me. The quality of the questions you ask and how you ask them will influence the franchisor about you in their evaluation of you, and their responses to your questions will influence your decision about proceeding with them.

CHAPTER 12

HEAR FROM AN ALREADY SUCCESSFUL FRANCHISEES

The Best Advisor Is Someone Who's Done It Before

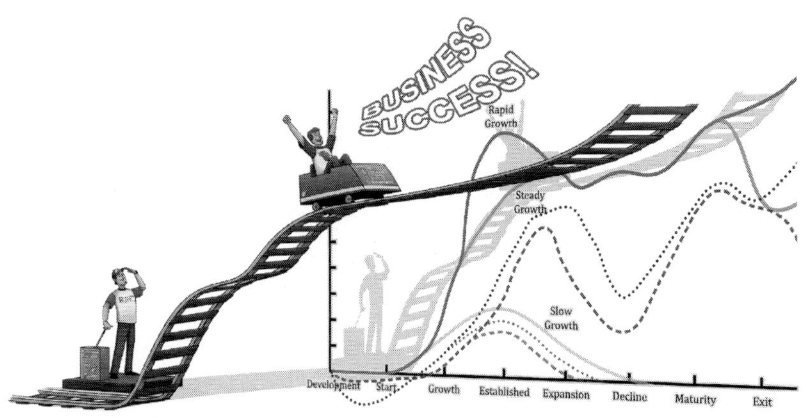

"One of the greatest values of mentors is the ability to see ahead what others cannot see and to help them navigate a course to their destination."

—John C. Maxwell

Why the Best Advisor Is Someone Who's Done It Before?

There has been significant research done among entrepreneurs, asking them whose advice they trust most when faced with critical issues affecting their business. The most recent survey I was involved in conducting on this topic revealed that entrepreneurs put the most faith in the advice of fellow business owners (31%), more than business coaches (24%) or consultants (4%). Additionally, when entrepreneurs do hire a business coach, 73% seek out someone who has owned their own business.

75% of business owners face the same challenges, regardless of size or industry. With fellow business owners ranking as the single-most trusted advisor, it's clear entrepreneurs are seeking advice from someone who is current, in the field and whose motivation for giving advice isn't personal or professional gain.

It is for this reason that I reached out to business owners that have been franchisees, and it is these franchisees that I know and have been successful within their respective franchise businesses and they are franchisees that I admire.

I believe in mentoring, and although mentoring is normally conducted one-on-one, the lessons you will learn from this chapter speak to anyone considering becoming a franchisee from people that have been there and have experience to share for your benefit. There are many definitions of mentoring. However, the most succinct definition of mentoring is when someone shares their knowledge, skills and experience to help another person progress. What they're often saying is, 'I've been where you are or where you're going; I've had experiences both good and bad and I'd like to share them with you so that you can learn from my experiences for your benefit'.

I have played around with who I put first, I tried to rank them, but the reality is that they are all impressive franchisees, and all have something memorable and worthwhile to share with anyone considering franchising. Trying to allocate position in this chapter was like picking between your children and reminded me of the biblical tale in the 'Judgement of Solomon'.

I believe you will find nuggets of gold in the following chapter: principles and suggestions from those that have gone before you that will make your journey into franchising smoother and hopefully lead to similar levels of success that the contributors to this chapter have done in their franchised businesses.

Peter Elligett

I first met Peter Elligett when I was 16 years old, and Peter was one of the managers I had at McDonald's. Peter was 'fast tracked' through the McDonald's system as a standout executive. After seven years with McDonald's, Peter finished up as a franchise consultant and became a franchisee with Amber Tiles. Peter was the first franchisee with Amber Tiles, so he has experience with an emerging franchisor brand. After achieving much success with Amber Tiles, Peter took on a national role with franchisor Cookie Man with the view of buying the business from the owner. For the next 11 years, he owned and operated the business in Australia and expanded the brand into India and other parts of the world through a franchising model.

His business was acquired by private equity, and he joined Allied Brands, who had acquired the Cookie Man brand as an executive director. The brand was merged with Mrs Fields bakery café in 2010. Peter is now the CEO of the parent company for Mrs Fields, Cookies Australia, owns and operates a domestic home services franchise business as the franchisor and is also a shareholder and director in Franchise Ready.

As you can see from his history, Peter has held every possible role within the franchise sector management: as a franchise consultant, franchisee, franchisor, general manager, director and international franchisor. He has had private equity acquisition experience and been business owner. If it's happened in franchising, Peter has seen it, so he is well credentialed to share his thoughts and experiences on franchising and what it takes to be a successful franchisee, having worked with over 1,000 franchisees in his career.

1. Tell me about your franchise history, employment and franchise systems you have worked in or been a franchisee.

I worked at McDonald's for 10 years, starting on the fast-track graduate programme. I started as a trainee, second, first, store manager, company supervisor and franchise consultant.

Franchisee — Amber Tiles, along with another McDonald's senior manager — took on the first franchises for Amber Tiles. Operated and ran the number-one sales volume store in the portfolio.

Cookie Man — commenced as the franchise manager to general manager and then did a management buy-out of Cookie Man — partnering with investment bank Hill & Young. During my ownership, I had 60 retail stores in Australia, 64 in India (opened market in 1999 — largest Australian retailer in India), 14 in China, 14 in Greece, 2 in Cyprus, 2 in Egypt, Bahrain, Mexico, Argentina, Chile, Singapore and Thailand. I sold to Allied Brands Ltd in 2007.

I also started and built a biscuit contract manufacturing company called Ozzibik, making cookies, biscuits and functional foods for Coles, Woolworths, Qantas, Uncle Toby's, Arnotts and numerous other customers. Sold to Freedom Foods Ltd in 2007.

Executive director — Allied Brands Ltd.

CEO — Mrs Fields (including Cookie Man, which was purchased in 2010 by Mrs Fields).

Director and shareholder — Franchise Ready.

2. Why did you choose franchising as the vehicle for your business?

There is no doubt in my mind that franchisees, who have a significant proportion of their wealth tied up in a business, will generally provide better quality service, cleanliness and value to a customer than an employee of a business. Further, growing a retail business with like-minded, self-motivated individuals was more enticing than trying to grow with employees.

3. What successes have you had in your franchise journey (awards, lifestyle, what are you proud of?)

Over the years, there have been a lot of awards and accolades for the business, but truthfully, what gives me personal satisfaction is knowing that I have contributed opportunities for success, money, lifestyle, family, housing and education to hundreds of people. Most people that joined my franchise believed in me and my vision for the business. I always looked at the franchisees as my partners and took their investment in my company very personally. Not everyone succeeded, however, I believe that I have always supported our franchisees through the tough periods as well as the good.

4. What lessons have you learnt, any failures or mistakes made?

I have always been careful and cautious, and in hindsight, should have backed my own judgement over the Private Equity — investment gurus. If I could do it all again, I would have grown a lot faster, bought the industrial and retail real estate that I was using rather than rent and made successful growth acquisitions that presented over the years.

I would also hire the best financial team that I could get to provide accurate and timely financial data for the business and be ruthless in controlling debtors and cashflow.

5. What do you wish you had done before entering a franchise? What can prospective franchisees learn from your experience?

I was a highly experienced franchise executive when I became a franchisee, however, I lacked experience in the management of debtors and cashflow. If I was entering a franchise today, not only would I seek a competent franchise lawyer, but I would engage a franchise-experienced accountant to work through sales/profit projection scenarios and cashflow projections, set up accounting procedures for the business and do monthly P&Ls and cashflows to ensure that I knew what was happening in advance. In my experience, most franchisees do a yearly P&L and have very little understanding of the metrics of their business or the problems that they actually have. Many franchisees could have avoided failure if they had understood their financial position and taken remedial action before the problems became critical.

6. What makes a good franchisor?

Having a great business idea that is replicable, a passion for the business and the people in it, the ability to support and work with franchisees to constantly improve, honest and open communication at all times and listening for feedback from franchisees and staff.

Franchisors have to lead and adapt to ever-changing business conditions and show leadership in the good times and times of adversity.

In the end, it is up to the franchisor to engender a great culture (personal, brand, corporate and environmental values) that franchisees are proud to be a part of.

7. What makes a franchise system good?

The franchisor should have a strong and inclusive corporate culture that makes the franchisee proud to be part of. In my time with McDonald's, what separated them from other franchisors was a cohort of management and staff that lived and breathed the brand — a brotherhood/sisterhood of like-mind individuals that passionately strived for success. Other attributes that potential franchisees should look for are:

- For mature brands — a continuous track record of success, and for emerging franchisors — a steady but manageable improvement in unit revenue and unit numbers.
- Excellent, passionate leadership from the owner, CEO and management
- Thorough and professional initial and ongoing training
- Active, effective and well-trained field support
- Effective, qualified franchisee selection process. It is not good enough to just have the funds to join a network. The ultimate strength of a franchise organisation lies in the franchisees' drive to continually improve revenue, profitability and customer experience and to be a part of and drive the culture of the business.
- Excellent marketing and revenue generation strategies.

- A strong financial base — a drive for profitability for both the franchisee and franchisor
- Ongoing innovation
- Happy franchisees who promote the business.

8. What makes a good franchisee?

You need to be passionate about the brand that you are becoming a part of — live, breathe, learn and be a part of the franchisee community. Be prepared to change, adapt and encourage continual improvement. One of the best traits for a franchisee is resilience — being able to push through the challenges that invariably arise from day-to-day, especially in the establishment phase of the franchise business.

There is a myth about improving the quality of life in your own business — this can only be achieved by putting in the long hours and hard work to get to that place. In many cases, there are no sick days or holidays while the business gets established and to a point where you may be able to shorten your hours or take a day off — but the challenges can be worth it.

I think that in many cases, franchisees are reluctant to put up their hand for help or wait too long when problems arise. Most franchisors are equipped to deal with most problems that arise, and the benefit of being in a system is that there is always help at hand from management, field support or franchisee peers.

Having a strong financial base going into business is obviously a benefit, however, ensuring that you have accurate and timely financial data in your business is critical for success. If a franchisee does not understand the basics of profit and loss, balance sheet and cashflow, they should learn quickly or seek professional assistance to make sure the business is and remains profitable and viable.

9. What advice would you give a prospective franchisee?

If you want to buy a franchise in a particular system, look for all the attributes in the previous question. Further, I always recommend that the franchisee applicant does a minimum of three days of on-the-job experience with a franchisee to see if they enjoy the work and can ultimately see themselves in that environment. They should also talk, face to face, if possible, to as many franchisees as they can to try and get a picture of the franchisor, their management, field staff, innovation, profitability, hours worked, issues etc., before committing to a franchise.

Lastly, whilst it can be more costly at face value, seek professional advice from a franchise specialist lawyer and accountant. My experience is that in the long run, they will provide much more incisive and accurate advice and actually be less expensive in the long run or save you from potentially making a serious and costly mistake.

10. What does it mean to be 'invested' when it comes to franchising?

Going back to my previous points, being invested means being passionate about the franchise you are joining, learning as much as possible about the business before joining and committing to the success of the brand as well as your individual unit when you join. One of the greatest benefits of joining a franchise is that you are connected to a group of like-minded people and the business management team that are, hopefully, all pulling in the same direction.

Despite many articles to the contrary, franchisees are not helpless when a franchisor has lost their way — franchisees can engender change through consultation, franchise advisory councils etc. Using McDonalds' again as an example, many of the successful menu items and marketing programmes have been spearheaded by the franchisee group.

Ultimately, everything that a franchisee does for the system improves the culture, viability and value (for resales) of the system and individual franchise units.

Richard Kentwell

I met Richard Kentwell at McDonald's, he and I did all our training courses together, and every time, Richard was the guy that came first academically. Richard is super smart, both book-smart and from a practical perspective. Although we did all our training together and progressed through the ranks of McDonald's management, Richard did far more than me and, at one point, was my immediate supervisor when I was a restaurant manager. I had enormous respect for Richard at that time, and he went on to impress me even more through his career as a franchisee in multiple successful franchise brands. Richard was one of the first middle management team members at McDonald's to get the opportunity to become a McDonald's franchisee. After leaving McDonald's, Richard joined a small franchise system called Shakespeare Pies, where he grew that business to be the highest volume and most successful outlet in that group and was instrumental in assisting the franchisor in growing that brand. I've seen Richard overcome adversity and go on to be successful in every franchise business that he has been involved in. Richard is well qualified to share his franchising experience with aspiring franchisees.

Tell me about your franchise history, employment, franchise systems you have worked in or been a franchisee.

I started as a trainee manager with McDonald's in August 1984, and in 1991, was promoted to the franchise department as a business consultant. I stayed there until 1997 when I purchased the McDonald's franchise on Bondi Beach. I renovated, then sold the business in 2001, just after the Sydney Olympic Games.

In 2002, I opened a Shakespeare Pies and coffee franchise in the International Terminal at Sydney Airport (later renamed Jesters Pies) before it was closed in 2008 for the terminal renovation and security upgrade.

Between 2008 and 2015, I operated as a freelance business consultant, working primarily with the company that owned Jesters Pies and Krispy Kreme donuts. This involved relocating to Perth, and when my contract expired, my partner and I decided to settle permanently there.

In 2016, we took over the Guzman y Gomez store in Northbridge, which we continue to operate to this day.

Why did you choose franchising as the vehicle for your business?

I didn't deliberately choose franchising — it chose me! 'Growing up' in the fast-paced and rapidly growing McDonald's chain gave me an invaluable perspective into the franchising industry, and regardless of your views on the contribution it has made to the Australian culture, it was incredible business training. It's difficult not to apply the business principles learned during that time whenever a business opportunity presents itself.

What successes have you had in your franchise journey (awards, lifestyle, what are you proud of?)

There have been some tremendous highs and lows during this journey. Running a McDonald's outlet across the road from Bondi Beach, the beach volleyball venue during the 2000 Olympic Games, was a highlight. Building a successful pie and coffee business at Sydney Airport based on solid customer service was also rewarding. We've won a couple of customer service awards in our time with Guzman y Gomez and are currently upscaling the business to cope with the opening of the new university on the city block right behind us.

What lessons have you learnt, any failures or mistakes made?

The biggest heartbreak would be having to close the coffee shop at the airport when they renovated the terminal in 2008. Overnight, the asset became worthless when we were told that it wasn't being renewed. Six years of blood, sweat and tears down the drain and a very valuable lesson about the security of tenure when opening a business.

What do you wish you had done before entering a franchise? What can prospective franchisees learn from your experience?

Based on the previous response, clearly, the answer to this would have been confirming the security of tenure, either through a longer lease or options to renew. That may not have been an option, but perhaps in letting this site go, we may have opened another site with more long-term security.

What's the point of working hard to build a successful business if the landlord has you over their knee when renewal time comes? Landlords of certain well-known larger shopping centres have a reputation for this. When it comes time for renewal, they propose significant rent increases for the new lease term, knowing that failure to agree to these terms means rendering the business worthless.

What makes a good franchisor?

A good franchisor has the mindset that they can only succeed if the franchisees are successful and sets up a system to make this happen. Good communication, led by example, reward success and invest in the long-term growth of the business.

What makes a franchise system good?

It's hard to go wrong when the goals of the franchisor match the goals of the franchisee. As an example, how does the franchisor generate their income? If the bulk of their income is derived as a percentage of the franchisee's sales, that's a good sign. In general, the best way to improve profitability in a business is through consistent positive sales growth. If a franchisor is reliant on sales growth in the individual franchises to increase their own bottom line, they're more likely to make decisions for the entire business to achieve this.

What makes a good franchisee?

Fulltime involvement in the business(es), a passion for hard work and tremendous patience. In almost 40 years in the industry, I've realised that 'silver bullets' that transform businesses overnight almost never happen. The industry is, however, riddled with successful business owners that have worked their asses off, got to know their customers, become a part of their local community, and looked after the people they have working for them, year after year! It's hard for that not to pay off!

What advice would you give a prospective franchisee?

Do something you love or at least have a passion for.

Do your homework! What advantage am I getting from paying a franchisor for their brand (or product)? As an example, I've always struggled to understand the success of gym franchises. I know they can be successful, but what makes their product unique enough that if a competitor opened next door, customers would still want to pay to use my facilities over theirs? Same with juice bars. What makes one juice bar's blended juice and ice combination uniquely better than another that makes it worth paying a fee from your sales to the franchisor? How much is that brand recognition worth?

When opening the pie and coffee shop at Sydney Airport, I did due diligence and was reassured that the pies were the best I'd ever tasted, and the coffee they sold (Allpress) was one of the best on the market. It makes growing a business easier when your customers absolutely love the taste of your food!

It's the same reason I became a part of Guzman y Gomez. When researching the brand, I went to several of their outlets (and to their competitors) and was blown away by their almost religious attention to food taste, quality and culture. It was tough going in the first few years before the brand recognition lifted in Western Australia, but it was the constant complimentary feedback from my customers that reassured me that I was in the right game and on the right team!

What does it mean to be 'invested' when it comes to franchising?

Buying a franchise is not buying a job; it's buying into a lifestyle that requires passion, perseverance, patience and plain hard work. If you're not able to commit to that lifestyle choice, you're not invested!

Michael Sleiman

Some may call me biased as Michael is one of my closest friends, and I have known him since he was a crew member at Punchbowl McDonald's back in 1992. Michael progressed through the management ranks at McDonald's and operated at senior management within training and franchising departments before coming to work with me in other franchise businesses as a state and national franchise manager. Whilst his performance working in franchising as an executive is impressive, it's what he has done since starting his own business, a franchise with First National Real Estate group.

Michael has won more industry and franchise awards than I can recount and has built an amazing business. Michael has leveraged everything that he has learnt from his time in franchised businesses but has brought his own unique style, work ethic and values to contribute to his enormous success. Michael is one of the most generous people I know and was very happy to contribute to this chapter by sharing his experience and knowledge of franchising to the benefit of aspiring business owners considering franchising as their route to market.

1. Tell me about your franchise history, employment, franchise systems you have worked in or been a franchisee.

I started working for McDonald's at the age of 14 years and 6 months. Having started out as a casual employee working after school hours. Little did I know, 22 years on, I would climb the corporate ladder. My role started out as a junior employee, progressing to a crew trainer, crew chief, assistant manager, eventually becoming a restaurant manager at the age of 21.

This would then take me onto a training and development consultant working at the head office training facility. Four years on, my role transitioned into a company consultant, followed by a franchise consultant.

2. Why did you choose franchising as the vehicle for your business?

I personally didn't think at the time 'franchising' was a vehicle for my eventual business.

However, it was certainly a fantastic stepping stone to my goal to become a business owner in real estate, having joined a real estate franchise known as 'First National'.

In 2007, I took the big leap of faith, and after 23 years working for McDonald's, I decided it was time to back myself and start my own 'commission-only sales business'.

Without a doubt a huge change and risk because I was no longer being paid an income, no company car and all the perks that come with a paid salary package. I also had to sell my family home to look after my family and pay our bills.

3. What successes have you had in your franchise journey (awards, lifestyle, what are you proud of?)

I was very blessed to be able to achieve success in a very short period. At the time, I had no experience, I had no idea what the systems and processes were, and I was unknown to the local community.

Within nine months, I was the number-one selling agent within the office, within two years, I was among the top three selling agents in the district and by year three, I was ranked in the top ten agents in the First National network in NSW (which comprises approximately 400 agents in the NSW network). Later on, achieving many number-one awards in Australia for being the number one-selling agent in the network and the number-one auction agent in Australia six years in a row.

I'm most proud of the support my wife Paula gave me when we made the decision to start my own business. Without her support and trusting me, we would not be where we are today. I'm also proud of the reputation and support we have in the community today, sponsoring many local schools and sporting organisations in the district.

What lessons have you learnt, any failures or mistakes made?

There are many lessons I have learnt and mistakes made, however, I don't feel they are failures. Lessons and mistakes will always be made; to me, they are called 'learning' or 'gaining experience'. Making the same mistakes repetitively would be poor management or lack of care, and in my business, we care very much.

In my opinion, growth comes by learning from mistakes made. The biggest challenge business owners face today is staff management and client relationships.

The changes I have experienced over many years (particularly working with people at a high management level) are, without doubts, our number-one priority and certainly take up a lot of our time.

Constant support, care, counselling, mentoring on a regular basis in 2023 is very different compared to the past. Whilst I'm certainly not trying to sound negative, staff expectations and attitudes can be challenging at times and keeping them happy seem to take precedence.

4. What do you wish you had done before entering a franchise? What can prospective franchisees learn from your experience?

Having had 23 years of experience in the McDonald's franchise system, in my opinion, most probably the best franchise system in the world. I can honestly say it was the other way around.

I was able to implement structure and systems in my real estate career, which were, in many cases, non-existent.

My experience allowed me to exponentially grow at a rapid rate in a short period. The systems I had implemented also helped the business grow, and eventually, other staff members were able to gain the benefits of the improved systems.

If I was advising others before entering the franchise system, naturally working for or in a franchise system (a good system) as an employee would be a great start. If that's not possible, they must take advantage of the system and experienced staff members training and development support on a regular basis.

'Never be afraid to ask for help and support'.

5. What makes a good franchisor?

- Provides constant support.
- Listens to the franchisees.
- Offers ongoing training.
- Has a very good branding team.
- Has a very good marketing team.
- Has a very good operational consultant team.
- Works on relationships with franchisees.
- Provides regular training.
- Commits to marketing spend.
- Provides regular updates through communication materials.
- Has a least one–two conferences or franchise meetings per annum.

6. What makes a franchise system good?

- Historical evidence of success
- Great brand awareness

- Great ongoing marketing campaigns
- Regular internal support from the franchisor
- A franchisee's ability to work with other franchisees within the network
- Regular communication and training
- A support network offered, particularly when required by the franchisee and staff
- Franchise growth abilities, particularly if the franchisee can grow more stores
- Respecting district rules, meaning the franchisor doesn't damage other franchisee businesses by opening other stores and offering them to new franchisees.

7. What makes a good franchisee?

- Leadership
- Great people skills
- Great communication skills
- The ability to guide and support staff (not always just work related, mentoring)
- Surround yourself with a good network of qualified consultants, e.g., accountants, bookkeepers, legal advisors, franchise company consultants, training networks.
- Continue to provide training to staff on a regular basis.
- Be present in the business.
- Provide incentives, including bonus schemes.

8. What advice would you give a prospective franchisee?

- If you are going to a franchise system, make sure you have spoken to other franchisees.

- Spend time working in a store.
- Ensure you are provided with good training, including your future staff.
- Make sure you have read the agreement, obtain accounting and legal advice.
- Make sure you are not over-committed financially and be careful not to risk your most valuable assets as security.
- Ensure you have good cash flow, allow for a 12–24-month period for basic wages and little profit (if profitable in a short time).
- Reinvest back into the business and keep the business liquidity strong.
- Don't be afraid to ask for help.
- Have a good accountant and bookkeeper.
- Stay in regular touch with other franchisees, especially the successful ones.
- Make good use of training seminars.
- Regularly invite operational consultants into the business.

9. What does it mean to be 'invested' when it comes to franchising? As a franchisee, the buck stops with you. Yes, you are involved in a franchisee system, but let me be clear, the system is only as good as its owner/leader. Don't think for one second that by going into a franchise system, your life should be easier. It's not. If you are not actively involved in the business, you will run risks; if you don't show leadership, you will encounter problems; if you don't manage staff, they will leave. If you don't build a good inhouse culture, staff won't be happy. In truth, I can go on and on. I'll leave you with the following:

Happy franchisees should have happy staff; happy staff should have customers. Happy customers mean they come back. Do all you can to create a strong culture, and that culture starts with its leader, that is you, the franchisee!

David Ciantar

I guess the more you read this chapter, the more you will see that I have included many people that I have known, that have worked with me and that have McDonald's experience. There is a pattern here, and that's because of the positive experience that I had at McDonald's and the success that business has had as a franchise business. David worked with me as a manager in 1992, and he too had a successful career at McDonald's before going on to lead 10 franchise businesses in a senior leadership position. During this time, David purchased a franchise restaurant business and was recognised as rookie and franchisee of the year before selling the business and focusing on his fulltime career in franchising. David now heads up the business sales and franchising part of our business. David has worked with more franchisees than anyone I know; he's been a franchisee and worked in multiple franchised businesses and in our business, he has interviewed over 8,000 prospective franchisees, so he has a deep insight into what it means to be a franchisee and what it takes to be successful.

1. **Tell me about your franchise history, employment, franchise systems you have worked in or been a franchisee.**

My franchise journey commenced in 1997 when I was promoted to the franchising department of McDonald's Australia Limited. McDonald's has predominantly been known as one of the best franchisors in the country, and I was lucky enough to learn my skills running five company stores as a supervisor before gaining the skills to then transition into the franchising part of the company. This was an interesting part of the company, as 85% of the stores were franchised, and working with the franchisees was where you put your craft to the test.

Upon leaving McDonald's, I was then fortunate enough to work for several franchised brands who appreciated my skillset. Some of these companies include Telstra, New Zealand Natural, Cookie Man, Gloria Jean's Coffees, Anytime Fitness, Fastway Couriers, Pirtek Fluid Systems, Pizza Hut and Eagle Boys Pizza. The skills of managing franchisees were very transferrable, and I was lucky enough to be exposed to food retail, QSR, telco, transport, services and fitness.

In 2004, one of my best friends, Jeff, approached me to see if I was interested in investing in a franchise. We looked at many different types of franchise systems, reviewing financials, assessing franchisors and looking at potential. We got very close to purchasing two Red Rooster stores in food courts, but we decided against it, given the development in the two centres we were looking at. Then, we had another colleague of ours who invested in a Hog's Breath Cafe. At the time, the business was opening sites and starting to break in the restaurant/bar-type business. We looked at the financials closely and met with a number of franchisees. The feedback from the franchisees, as well as their casual approach, is what ultimately got us across the line. We had spoken to some local franchisees and found out that the Parramatta store was to be put on the market. The Parramatta store was a great opportunity for Jeff and me — given that it would be my first business venture with a partner — and Jeff's second business venture. We had decided early on that I would remain in fulltime employment, and that Jeff would be the nominated fulltime manager/operating partner. Jeff also had a distinguished career with McDonald's and had really wanted to leave and work for himself. He supervised five company-owned stores and wanted to do something for himself. His wife Ernestina was also extremely helpful, as she had carried out payroll and bookkeeping functions for a number of franchisees, and this really assisted us in the early stages of the business.

Hog's Breath Cafe was a relaxed system, and we had to work really hard to turn the business around. In the first year, we managed to receive Rookies of the Year award, and in the second year, we received Franchisees of the Year. The awards weren't something we really aspired to but nonetheless, nice to receive to reward our hard work. Jeff would pretty much work six–seven days a week, and I would work Friday and Saturday nights as well as help Jeff when there were some busier nights or functions. We made a great team for our two years together. It was a lot to do – holding down a fulltime role and having a business that I worked in as well. Jeff and I agreed that I would eventually exit the business, and that he would amicably buy my share. Not a lot of people can say that they are still friends with the ex-business partners. For us, it was straightforward. It was also great for Jeff and Ernestina to grow their business aspirations and take over another two stores with Hog's Breath. I was general manager of New Zealand Natural at the time and continued to stay in the franchising industry, moving to Cookie Man, Gloria Jean's Coffees, then Anytime Fitness.

Whilst I have been fortunate enough to learn from some successful franchisor organisations, I also learnt some quick lessons from the 'not-so-great' franchisors. Compliance and systems were always quite high on my agenda, as I learnt quickly that a franchisor could only be successful with amazing franchisees. For this reason, I really enjoyed my time at Anytime Fitness. It was a new brand coming to Australia from the USA. They commenced operations in Australia in late 2009. I heard that they were looking for a general manager in 2010 and applied for the position. My time at Anytime Fitness was extremely rewarding. I commenced with them, having five clubs opened, and just after my 2.5 years, opened a further 195 to reach 200. They are now the largest franchised fitness chain in all of Australia. I liked to think I played a part and left a small legacy towards their success. It was the only franchise system where we had more franchisees buying territories than available sites.

My career continues in the franchising industry, where I now assist franchisors in selling new sites and territories, as well as selling their existing stores and locations. Franchise Ready has provided outstanding consultancy to several franchise organisations throughout Australia, and to be heading up the recruitment team gives me an enormous amount of satisfaction. Being able to share your knowledge, learn from your pitfalls and challenge the franchisor's thinking is something that is really rewarding. I have had an enormous amount of pride working with some amazing new and emerging brands such as BCMC, Piccolo Me, Fat Jak's and Degani , to name a few.

Having held several roles as a general manager, director, head of and C-suite positions has allowed me to understand what great franchising is all about as well as understand the main priorities for franchisors when growing. In my 30 years of working in franchising, you quickly learn about the priorities for a franchisee and how you can play a part in their success.

2. Why did you choose franchising as the vehicle for your business?

There is something about franchising that draws my interest. I get the opportunity to work with some amazing founders and senior management, whilst playing a part in the organisation's growth. Franchising makes sense to many companies on so many levels. It does not only provide the vehicle for growth but also the opportunity for a brand to excel and scale quite rapidly. Once a founder, director or CEO understands what they need to do to commence franchising, the company can really become slick, systemised and polished for franchisees to adapt.

3. What successes have you had in your franchise journey (awards, lifestyle, what are you proud of?)

I have been lucky enough to receive several awards for my work in franchising, but for me, it's more about the general achievement of working with various brands that really gives me a great deal of satisfaction. One of the most satisfying roles I had was when I was appointed as general manager for Anytime Fitness, back in May 2010. When I joined the franchisors — the brother and sister team, Justin and Jacinta McDonnell — they had five clubs opened, with a number planned in terms of territory sales. It was unbelievably rewarding to take Anytime Fitness to 200 clubs in just two years. This was a massive achievement, given that we had to build a leasing and property team as well as add to our operations team to support the clubs that were opening. The thrill of opening clubs (sometimes two–three in one week) was enormously satisfying. It didn't take long for people in the franchising and fitness industry to stand up and take note. It was an amazing time to be part of such an iconic brand.

Another moment that I was extremely proud of was the opportunity to work with Pizza Hut Australia and Allegro Funds and assist with the transition of Eagle Boys stores to Pizza Hut. This was an amazing opportunity to work with some very talented people and be part of something special. Back in 2016, Yum! — the owners of Pizza Hut Australia —sold the business to Allegro Funds — a private equity company — who, along with some former McDonald's executives, had taken over the ownership and management. My role was to work with the Eagle Boys franchisees and transition at least 50 stores across to Pizza Hut. This role was extremely challenging yet rewarding. We generally closed an Eagle Boy's store on a Thursday night and reopened it on a Monday as a Pizza Hut store. The planning of this had to be meticulous to plan for things like signage, suppliers, branding, uniforms and store entity. I managed to obtain 57 stores during this process which essentially gave Pizza Hut another 20% of growth and an increase in market share.

4. What lessons have you learnt, any failures or mistakes made?
I think when I bought my first franchise with Hog's Breath Cafe, I could have done more research into the franchisor to fully understand their five-year plan and growth strategy. Whilst I don't regret my time joining Hog's Breath Cafe, I do believe it would have been nice to be armed with a bit more information.

I also could have planned to have a little more capital put aside, but I was lucky at the time that I kept my fulltime role and kept working whilst owning the franchise. The money side of the business was an extremely fast lesson to learn about cashflow and sales. We were fortunate that our sales were increasing and that the business was moving in the right direction. Had our sales been flat, we would have naturally needed some further funds. These types of lessons aren't ones that any university will teach you. They are really business fundamentals that you learn whilst owning a business.

5. What do you wish you had done before entering a franchise? What can prospective franchisees learn from your experience?

Research, research and more research. You can never be armed with enough information. The general franchise applicant I speak to today is quite franchise savvy, has generally spoken to other franchise brands and understands a lot more about franchising than when I was looking at one. My research was really about the franchisor sites, rent and financial performance. I also spoke to a couple of franchisees in the system I bought into, and I wish I had spoken to a few more that were around for a longer period. There can tend to be some attitudes toward more experienced franchisees. But I would strongly recommend talking to franchisees that have been in a system for over 5–10 years, as their experiences and knowledge would be second to none. The more you ask, the more you learn. This type of information from franchisees in a system can really address most of your underlying questions. Due diligence is a big thing that is pushed throughout the franchising industry. We have an information spread put out by the ACCC, which is an Information Statement for Prospective Franchisees. This is a four-page guide on the issues to consider before purchasing a franchise. Something like this wasn't available when I was looking around at a different number of franchisors. All this information assists in determining if purchasing a franchise is right for you.

6. What makes a good franchisor?

I'm often asked about 'What makes a good franchisor?', and from personal experience, there are several things that really stand out. Here is a list of the eight main points I believe make a good franchisor:

- The franchisor has really thought about their business and has a sound financial model.
- They demonstrate a great ability in what success looks like in their own business (first few outlets/ operations).
- They have a priority to communicate with their franchisees often and taken feedback on a multitude of issues.
- They think ahead looking at their uniqueness and what they are doing to be better than their competitors.
- They must have a plan, two-, five- and ten-year plan. What is ahead for the franchisor? Great franchisors really know where they want to be in years ahead.
- They have an underlying attention to franchisee profitability and sales. The good franchisors make this look like second nature and continuously draw their attention to how to control costs and increase sales and profits.
- They know their numbers. Great franchisors will understand their business so well that the numbers are some key selling points about their franchise model.
- They carry out their business practices, morally and ethically. Franchising has a lot of compliance behind it, and good franchisors have this well covered and part of their everyday business.

7. What makes a franchise system good?

Some may say that if a franchise system can last within its first two years, it is doing well. But a good franchise system is one that is adaptable and one that can pivot quickly. We have recently seen in 2021–22, with the Covid pandemic, just how many franchise systems did this well and others that probably didn't do enough. Good franchise systems will have a plan for various external factors that will affect their business operations and adapt to the economic climate at a cracking pace. Several franchisors invested early in required support and operations to ensure that they are sustainable and survive anything that is thrown at them. During the Covid pandemic, we saw lots of challenges with supply chain, pricing, staffing, trading and general operations. The good franchise systems were able to quickly adapt to these challenges and carry on with a positive approach to making business 'as usual' as possible.

8. What makes a good franchisee?

In my daily discussions with franchise applicants, there could be a never-ending list, but if you were to look at what a franchisor expects and what makes a franchisee good, then the below 10 points would certainly be a good indication of what a good franchisee looks like.

- A franchisee that isn't afraid to invest in their business.
- Someone who will hire great and extraordinary people to join their team.
- Someone who knows their numbers and continuously assesses their performance.
- A person who can look at growth and wants to expand on what they may presently have.
- Someone who can calculate the risks and rewards and assesses each situation carefully for a positive outcome.
- A person who will look at the debt and want to pay off their loans appropriately.

- A person who is dedicated to training and looks at their staff as being an investment.
- A person who will invest back into their business for all the right reasons.
- A person who is in touch with their customers and understands their needs.
- A person who has high standards both in quality, customer services and general cleanliness in their business. Staff and customers can tell this immediately.

9. What advice would you give a prospective franchisee?

Buying a franchise can be the second most expensive purchase you may make after a house. I would personally recommend that you go into this process with 'eyes wide open' and have a list of things you need to have answers for. Talking to the franchisor and a staff member just isn't enough. Looking at the competitors, talking to other franchisors, looking at where they are in comparison to their competitors and what their plans are — is a great start. Understanding the financials is one thing, but understanding the model and what can affect the franchise is also highly recommended. Don't invest in anything that you aren't fully aware of and ensure you take on all the information and ask 'Why?' and 'How?'. Information to invest in various franchisors is readily available, and it has never been safer to invest in a franchise. Talking to brokers, consultants, and coaches like Franchise Ready can assist you in your decision. Sometimes the best questions and talking points are the ones that others bring to your attention.

10. What does it mean to be 'invested' when it comes to franchising?

Sure, there is a financial capability of investing in a franchise brand, but 'invested' can also mean the connection you have with that brand also.

Apart from being financially invested, a franchisee is certainly 'emotionally invested', too. They have feelings, lifestyle and family that are attached to this as well. Being invested also means that you would be looking for a return, but the 'invested' component is also how much dedication and commitment you put into a brand. Along with this type of invested dedication and commitment is also the blood, sweat and tears that people won't tell you about. Your total invested interest also needs to take your internal and external factors of life into consideration. When purchasing a franchise, you not only become part of a franchise organisation or family, but it becomes something that you need to believe in. Being invested in a franchise brand also means that you need to share the passion, vison and dreams of the franchisor and do your bit to ensure you are successful.

Steve & Tanya Palmer

I met Steve and Tanya Palmer when they approached us to help them franchise their Wingtopia business. I had heard of them because of my relationship with the Foodco business which operates Jamaica Blue café, which Steve and Tanya were very successful franchisees of, although they weren't there when I was a director, I heard lots of good things about them as franchisees.

The thing I love about them is that they have been successful in multiple franchise systems and have used franchising as a way for them to develop their portfolio of businesses and experiences. They have worked with three successful franchise systems and multiple stores within those systems operating in both regional and metropolitan areas. This grounding in business achieved through their experiences as franchisees and across multiple franchise systems has positioned them to be franchisors of their own business, Wingtopia.

For a lot of franchisees, franchising is their entry and exit to business ownership but there are a number of people that use franchising with experienced and established brands to develop their own skills so they can move on and do their own thing, a number of successful franchisees go on to create their own franchise systems leveraging what they learnt from their own franchisee experiences and this learning positions them well to understand what a franchisee needs, this is why I was so keen to have Steve and Tanya contribute to this section of the book.

1. **Tell me about your franchise history, employment, franchise systems you have worked in or been a franchisee.**

- Subway between 2005 to 2008. Opened the Subway store in Broome WA from new.
- Jamaica Blue Midland Gate and West Leederville between 2008 to 2012. These were brand new builds.
- Chicken Treat we opened and operated various regional and metropolitan stores as well as operating a mobile food van all operating across the entire state of WA and NT

2. **Why did you choose Franchising as the vehicle for your business?**

- We chose franchising for various reasons;
- as it was able to provide training
- To provide business systems both operational and financial
- To use recognisable brands that are safe and which you as a person align your values with.

3. What successes have you had in your franchise journey (Awards, lifestyle, what are you proud of?)

- Won national marketing award (Golden Bean award) within Jamaica Blue for highest coffee sales and quality of product.
- Chicken Treat we were part of an immersion team which provided direction for marketing into the future.
- Sat on the franchise advertising board for Chicken Treat making decisions for future advertising.

4. What lessons have you learnt, any failures or mistakes made?

- Not to micromanage staff
- Encourage staff to take ownership of the store.
- Encourage staff to make decisions within their skope of employment.
- As a franchisee, learn to delegate.
- Take time off regularly.
- Learn to pay yourself first.
- Have an exit strategy.

5. What do you wish you had done before entering a franchise? What can prospective franchisees learn from your experience?

- Ensure you are aware of all your legal rights and obligations under the franchise agreement.
- You need to ensure that if you are not comfortable with any items in the franchise agreement that you ask for clarification and change if you are not comfortable with the wording.
- Be prepared to walk away if you are not comfortable with the agreement.

6. What makes a good franchisor?

- One that is transparent and willing to listen to franchisees who are on the ground.
- Being prepared to make changes where change is required.
- Do not be dictatorial.
- Work together as a team franchisor and franchisee as one supportive team

7. What makes a franchise system Good?

- One that is transparent, a good listener and one that values their franchisees.

8. What makes a good franchisee?

- Someone who is willing and eager to learn.
- Excited about the brand
- Is positive.
- Able to solve problems on their own.

9. What advice would you give a prospective franchisee?

- Be open to learn.
- Do not be too hard on themselves.
- It is a journey.
- Do not be afraid to ask for help.

10. What does it mean to be 'invested' when it comes to franchising?

- Taking ownership
- Being proud of the brand
- Be willing to see it grow and to grow in the process.
- Work hard to see you and the brand grow.

Janiene Pollock

Yes, another McDonald's person, but this one has a very different experience to share with us, I worked with Janiene and her husband David when I worked at McDonald's, and together, they make a formidable couple and amazing franchisees. Both Janiene and David were extremely successful moving through the ranks at McDonald's in middle management with responsibility for company stores, training department and franchised stores. Janiene and David were some of the first middle management executives to leave the safety of McDonald's to pursue their dream of business ownership, and they operated many successful franchises across multiple brands. But their dream was to always return to McDonald's and become franchisees in the system they grew up in as kids and young adults.

1. Tell me about your franchise history, employment, franchise systems you have worked in or been a franchisee.

My introduction to franchising began as a 14-year-old when I got my very first job at McDonald's. I worked in a corporate store and climbed the corporate ladder over the next 17 years. I also had the experience of the role of franchise consultant, working directly with McDonald's licensees. My husband, David, also grew up with the Maccas system, having worked 22 years with both a licensee, and for the latter part of his career, he joined the corporation.

In the mid-'90s, when opening a new McDonald's store at Castle Hill, a new franchise opened in the food court that took my eye. This was well before Aussies went out for coffee or we had dedicated coffee houses. It was Gloria Jean's Coffees, and I was immediately addicted to the coffee. After investigation, I was contacted by the franchisor to see if we would like to take on a new franchise store no. 22 — Westfield Burwood. After some research and speaking to the banks, we decided to take the plunge and open up our very first franchise business — Burwood Gloria Jean's Coffees (this all happened in a five-week period). It was a whirlwind experience, and within the next 12 months, we opened another two stores at Merrylands and Wetherill Park. It was an amazing experience working with a relatively new franchisor after growing up in the world's best franchise system of McDonald's. We were able to take a lot of our learnings from McDonald's and help mould the systems and introduce suppliers for Gloria Jean's.

I then went on the search for the next challenge. I noticed a gap in the market for female-only gyms. There was no way I would open my own branded gym with zero fitness background. I joined the local Fernwood at Parramatta to do some research from a consumer's point of view. Impressed by its offering, I thought the business model had merit. I reached out to the franchisor for information, all whilst looking for the perfect location. David and I found a great building suitable for an 840-square Fernwood at Castle Hill. We began the process with the franchisor to become approved franchisees. The first real challenge we faced was rejection from the bank; this was by CBA — my childhood bank — they refused to support our business proposal. I clearly remember the bank manager telling me we would go broke because 'all gyms go broke', referring to the '80s. I swiftly closed all my accounts with CBA and transferred to Westpac, after receiving finance approval from them to build our first Fernwood at Castle Hill. It was a success; in fact, the most successful opening of a Fernwood for its time. We opened the gym, cashflow positive from day one. We were away, not that we had any gym/fitness background, so we put all the knowledge and systems we learnt from McDonald's into running the gym. Not long after, the

Parramatta facility came up for sale. We knew the potential it had, so took on the challenge, reinvested in a full-fit out and new equipment, and success!

Our lifelong family dream was always to come back to Maccas, the system we love and grew up with. After 12 years of running the coffee shops and gyms, we were afforded the opportunity to become a McDonald's franchisees. We sold the coffee shops and gyms and returned to Maccas, relocating our family and lives to WA to purchase two McDonald's stores — Riverton and Willetton. 2022 was my 10-year anniversary as an official McDonald's licensee. We love the system and hope to grow our portfolio in the coming years.

2. Why did you choose franchising as the vehicle for your business?

Franchise is the world we have grown up in since the age of 14. I feel the franchise model means we are stronger together, systems are provided, suppliers sorted, the formula and systems are there for you to run with and follow. The franchisor is like a safety net providing support and, importantly, protecting the brand for all partners. Although you are a business owner, you have the power of the brand, not to mention the financial backing to market the brand, unlike if you were in business alone. It is an incredible advantage.

3. What successes have you had in your franchise journey (awards, lifestyle, what are you proud of?)

During our time at Gloria Jean's Coffees, we won many small business awards, marketing awards etc. We also received many local business awards for Fernwood, including Business of the Year for the Parramatta region.

McDonald's is a very inclusive partnership. I represent the Western Australia licensees on the Senior Leadership Group, the Australian Leadership Group, the National Marketing Committee, the Sponsorship Committee. I am also honoured to be appointed to the Board of Ronald McDonald House Charities Western Australia (RMHCWA). I chaired the board for five years and now am a director. I have recently been appointed to the National Ronald McDonald House Australian Board of Directors.

My McDonald's business allows me the flexibility to participate in these committees and really give back to our charity. I currently chair the Western Australia Ride for Sick Kids, a bike ride raising much-needed funds for RMHCWA. Last ride, we had 40 riders riding from Margaret River back to Perth, raising over $500 thousand.

I have received many awards during our tenure to date with Maccas, including the most prestigious award — the Three-legged Stool Award — one voted on by your peers for contribution to the system.

4. What lessons have you learnt, any failures or mistakes made?

We have learnt lots of lessons on our journey with three different franchise partners. Regardless of the business, all businesses are people businesses. People are the key to success. Don't be afraid to surround yourself with people that are better than you. You cannot be an expert at all. You need to have a strong bond and transparent relationship with your franchisor. After all, they are your partner in business.

5. What do you wish you had done before entering a franchise? What can prospective franchisees learn from your experience?

We have been very happy with our due diligence and research before purchasing each of the businesses, I don't think we would change a thing. David and I work really well together — I am the risk-taker, and he is my hand brake, so to speak! We have clear, defined roles in the business — it is super important for a happy life at home and, more importantly, for our people in the workplace.

6. What makes a good franchisor?

Honesty, transparency, clear communication, partnership, win-win attitude. A desire for the franchisor to support and want for the franchisees to succeed.

7. What makes a franchise system good?

Working together to make the system stronger and more successful for both the franchisor and franchisee.

8. What makes a good franchisee?

A real belief in the franchise that you are purchasing and about to partner with.

A can-do attitude, not afraid to get in and do the hard yards. Must be a people person — you deal with people, as employees and customers will be critical to your success.

9. What advice would you give a prospective franchisee?

Do your research, try before you buy, talk to other franchisees, and ensure you can finance the deal, get a good accountant. Budget for the worst case and don't expect to have the same lifestyle as franchisees that may have been around for a very long time and are successful. It is hard work, and nothing comes easy. You really need to set goals and review them. Sounds strange, but also have the endgame in mind — what and when will be your exit strategy?

10. What does it mean to be 'invested' when it comes to franchising?

'Invested' means being invested not only financially. It is probably one of the biggest decisions you will ever make for you and your family. You simply can't expect to buy the franchise, and it will start to make you money and give you a lifestyle. It takes hard work, dedication and commitment. In the early days, your time can be one of the biggest investments you will make in the business. This could be a sacrifice to your current lifestyle and family time. I believe that you need to be passionate and truly believe in the brand that you are about to partner with. In the case of McDonald's, many of the licensees have been a partner with the system for well over 20 years.

Crystal Petzer

My first encounter with Crystal was when she applied for a franchise with The Alternative Board, which I was the franchisor for in Australia. I nearly didn't reach out to her and follow up on her enquiry because she was already a franchisee with two franchises with Hire A Hubby, a handyman trades business, and I thought, how could a tradie be a business coach and how could she do it when she already had two franchises. So, I did some research on Crystal and discovered the amazing pedigree she had in business and franchising through being a franchisee, and it got me thinking that she would be an amazing mentor because she has operated in multiple franchise businesses and established her own independent businesses. The beauty of franchising is that you don't have to be a technician or expert in the technical aspect of a business because a good franchise system can teach a franchisee how to be successful, and Crystal had already proven how successful she could be, wining multiple Franchisee of the Year awards within her chosen franchises and the ultimate recognition as the Franchise Council of Australia (FCA) Franchisee of the Year award winner. Crystal has worked across white-collar, blue-collar and retail franchise brands and brings a unique perspective to franchising and to the benefit of those considering franchising as their way to enter business ownership.

1. Tell me about your franchise history, employment, franchise systems you have worked in or been a franchisee.

My father owned a BP franchise in South Africa before we moved to Australia. Once here, he took on a commission-only franchise with Amoco Fuel in Dee Why, NSW in 1982. I worked with him in the business, helping with the Avis car hire and serving customers. Later, he obtained a franchise with Caltex in North Ryde, and I eventually got my own Caltex convenience store in Manly, NSW in 1994. Eventually, I owned and operated three Caltex service stations on the Northern Beaches.

In 2003, I began working for Caltex's head office as a category manager for eight years. My role involved managing relationships with suppliers and contracts, as well as overseeing various categories such as tobacco, bakery and confectionery. The position was a national role, which required me to work with retail franchisees and attend yearly franchisee conferences. During this time, my partner ran our Manly Caltex franchise, which we later sold.

While working for Caltex, we decided to leave our Manly franchise and pursue a new opportunity. In 2009, we acquired a franchise with Hire A Hubby in Narrabeen, and five years later, we added a second territory in Mona Vale. We still have the Mona Vale franchise and sold Narrabeen in 2020.

In 2018, I purchased a franchise with The Alternative Board, after selling an admin and bookkeeping business that I had started. I am still a member of The Alternative Board franchise network today, five years later.

Additionally, I have been a member of the FCA and served as a committee member for the NSW chapter.

2. Why did you choose franchising as the vehicle for your business?

When I started with Caltex, my focus was on utilising my existing skills, and at that time, service stations were a profitable venture. With my father's assistance, I could secure a franchise, as women were not typically given petrol franchises in those days. Having worked under my dad, I had a lot of relevant experience to draw upon.

We opted for Hire A Hubby because Jim wanted a hands-on job, and we were already familiar with franchising, so we knew it would be beneficial to have the franchise's support and established systems to speed up the process of getting started. Additionally, we enjoy attending conferences and having a team of fellow franchisees for help or guidance. This decision proved to be a successful one.

The primary reason I chose to join The Alternative Board franchise was to be a part of a larger group. Being international was very appealing. Additionally, I did not want to reinvent the wheel by creating my own systems and processes. Finally, I needed to learn quickly about being a business coach, and I felt that this franchise was the ideal platform to do so.

3. What successes have you had in your franchise journey (awards, lifestyle, what are you proud of?)

At the beginning of the franchise with Caltex, I was one of three female franchisees. The oil industry was always traditionally very male dominant; this has changed a little in later years, but I was very proud that they allowed me to take on the Manly site.

We have won several awards in the Caltex franchise. They ran a great program called All-Stars, and we won these three times for being one of the best franchisees with regards to doing well in the All-Stars Program. What I loved most about this franchise was that the service station allowed me the flexibility to take school holidays and gave us a great lifestyle at the time.

With Hire A Hubby, we have won Franchisee of the Year twice in 2016 and 2018. In 2019, we won FCA Franchisee of the Year — this was a big deal. Jim has won most valuable franchisee a couple of times, too. This business has been amazingly profitable and successful. We have had a great lifestyle of work balance with this business, which is what we wanted. Out of having the Hire A Hubby franchise, I started the admin and bookkeeping business which I was very proud of and helped many other franchisees by doing their admin for them. It was a very new concept for Hire A Hubby in those days.

The Alternative Board is relatively small, and the awards are about sales and our culture statement around CALIBER, but have won once in 2020 a CALIBER award.

4. What lessons have you learnt, any failures or mistakes made?

We sure made quite a few mistakes and had a few failures, too.

One failure was the Narrabeen Caltex site, which was always a very slow revenue generator, and we lost a significant amount of money in six months due to low sales. Our fixed costs, which were hard to reduce, were a bad combination for this site and I believe unless we were behind the counter and doing all the roles ourselves you could never make money. We had given it back to Caltex but lost our money. Good lesson that not all sites are busy and profitable.

At the end of our Caltex franchise, the oil company, had put up their franchise fees and commissions, and it was very hard to make money after paying them their share. I believe Ampol/Caltex Australia, having gone as a public company, changed the culture of the business, and it became focused on their shareholders and less on their franchisees.

With Hire A Hubby taking on a second franchise was more difficult than expected as you have to have two of everything in systems, like two Xeros, two Salesforce CRMs etc. The complexity of this almost makes having two franchises not worth it, however, we managed it for five years and got both franchises up doing around $500 thousand each per month. There was not much support from the head office as there was only two other franchisees nationally that had two franchises. This was not their focus.

Hire A Hubby changed their salesforce CRM (we use this for invoicing, scheduling and quoting), around four years ago to a newer version, which meant a new platform, and the changeover was difficult for us as we lost a lot of workarounds and information we had in place to make our businesses run well. Also, all the information did not come over into the new system. The lesson learnt from this was that the franchisor needed to consult with the franchisees on their systems and workarounds, however, we probably did not have much say on the change and could have asked more questions. This set us back for at least a year, since there were many bugs that needed to be fixed etc. I think both Hire A Hubby and the franchisees were happy when finally the new program was sorted out. This was very distracting to our business and stressful. The larger revenue-generating franchisees were the most impacted and the ones who used the systems to their full capacity.

The Alternative Board — my lessons here have been a few over the Covid and post-Covid times. It is important to continually look for new leads and have a system in place. Sometimes, when you have enough clients, you stop looking for new ones, but this is the wrong thing to do. You need to have a good lead-generating system that you always focus on to keep new clients coming through; it's really hard to start the sales process over when you have stopped it.

5. What do you wish you had done before entering a franchise? What can prospective franchisees learn from your experience?

With the Caltex franchise, I think we should have sold about four years before our franchise ended. We would have made more money that way. But I think we thought a good thing would go on forever — which was a bit naïve and we should all be aware that bad times and good times always happen in business. It is not always good to stay to the very end.

Don't go into the franchise heavily in debt; it is good to come in with enough cashflow and not fund all the business on credit. This allows the business to grow and gives you space to adjust to the lower profits when starting out.

With any franchise, you are buying the systems and the knowledge, and it is up to you to make this work. If you don't put in the effort to make it work, it will not work as well as you would hope for.

Knowing the track record of a franchise is also an important thing. The franchisor should have an office that is not a home office. This shows a commitment that they are serious about their franchise to work and have the space for staff and franchisees to visit.

6. What makes a good franchisor?

- The franchisor must be driven to succeed but also have people skills that enable them to support their franchisees.
- Franchisors also need to be thick-skinned, as you will meet different kinds of franchisees, which will test them. They need to be able to move through this without letting a minority ruin a good franchise. As the franchise grows, there will always be a percentage of difficult franchisees and good franchisees.
- Once the franchise is optimal, the franchisor needs to be able to maintain the core of the business and continue to improve the business systems etc., to stay relevant, which can be hard as most franchisees will want the system to stay the same, but this may not be good for future business.
- Being a leader and being able to take people on a journey.
- Have a great lead-generating system that produces good-quality leads.

7. What makes a franchise system good?

- All franchises should have a company-owned franchise area/store, but the franchisor should not be running this own on their own. This way, the company will understand what the franchisees are experiencing customers, leads, systems etc.
- The franchise must be proven it can work profitably — not just a company-run area but have several successful franchisees that have been doing it well and using the systems.
- The franchise has a good one-year and five-year direction and plan.
- Must have solid brand rules.
- Must have a successful lead generator that benefits all franchisees and business overall.

8. What makes a good franchisee?

- Not over-the-top entrepreneurial — otherwise, the rules and systems will be too confining for them.
- Have a great attitude and want to make their business successful.
- Have enough cash and support from family — often it gets hard and they will need to have that support to see them through.
- If franchisee has a glass-half-empty view of life, franchising will be hard for them, as you need that optimism and belief in yourself to be able to succeed.
- Be a great people person — as you need to wear all the hats in the business in the beginning so that means you need to be able to do sales and maintain relationships with clients, staff, franchisor.

9. What advice would you give a prospective franchisee?

- Check out the franchisor first:
    - Do they have an office?
    - How long has the business been going for? Less than two years — not sure what you are buying? There needs to be a track record; how many are company-run areas, stores? Do they have any?
    - Can you get easy access to the franchisor? You need to know them, not just their staff as they are the decision-makers.
    - Are they part of the FCA? Often, in the beginning, they feel that this is too expensive, but if they are not part of an industry body, it seems like they are not serious about the quality of the management and being part of the larger franchise community.
    - Website and lead generator — if the franchise does not have a good website and lead generator, why is that? Often, this

makes it hard to get going if they have worked this out for your area. If they have one, make sure you confirm with existing franchisees that this is the case.

- Always ring three or four franchisees, not just the ones they recommend and ask them the following:
    - How long have they been in the franchise?
    - What do they like about the franchise?
    - How much support do they get?
    - What are the things that they would like to improve in the franchise?
    - What advice would they give you coming into the franchise?
    - Why do they stay?

10. What does it mean to be 'invested' when it comes to franchising?

- You need to like the brand and the people in the franchise; if you don't, you will find this will get irritating and be a problem for you down the track.
- Do you like the other franchisees and culture of the franchise? If not, because you will be working and talking with these people, having a franchise is not for a lone ranger; the value is being part of the brand and franchise.
- You need to love the work you will be doing in your new franchise.
- Are you invested for five years to make a go of your new business — if not, what are the reasons you are joining?
- What are your plans for next five years or more? This is going to be hard work to get it off the ground if a new area or store.

CHAPTER 13

THE QUESTIONS TO ASK

This Is the Most Important Step in the Process

Questions to Ask When Interviewing Franchisors

1. How did the franchise get started, and what is the background of your executives?

- Who were the founders?
- Are the founders still involved?
- What was their motivation for starting the business?
- Have the franchisor shared the organisational chart, who the support team is and what is their experience?

Ask yourself if you possess similar skill sets and a passion for the industry.

Finding the perfect match requires not only that you feel the franchisor has adequate experience, but that you identify with the fundamentals of the business.

2. What are your criteria for choosing a franchisee?

Franchisors typically have a list of qualifications and personality traits that fit best with their brand. It's important to investigate those criteria and determine whether you feel your personality and skill set fit within the system.

- Does the franchisor use a franchise behavioural profiling tool, and have they mapped the attributes of their ideal franchisee?
- Does the franchisor have an established recruitment process/map which outlines the steps in the recruitment process?
    - Who are their best franchisees?
    - Why are they the best franchisees?
    - Is there a multi-site franchise opportunity?

3. How much do I have to invest before I can open my doors?

The initial investment for starting a franchise can vary from a few thousand dollars to more than a million. The franchise agreement lists the fixed dollar amounts, including the franchise fee, training fee, legal expenses and ongoing fees, such as franchise royalties and marketing costs. The FDD details additional startup costs, such as real estate, equipment, licenses etc. Be sure to discuss these items in depth with the franchisor so that you have a clear understanding of your investment and what you will need financially to get up and running.

Ask the franchisor:

- Do they have a financial modelling tool so that you can evaluate the establishment costs, potential revenue scenarios and potential return on capital?
- Is there a chance of a budgeted cost overrun?

- What are the deposit requirements, and is this refundable?
- How much time do I need to invest in training, set-up and the discovery process before the franchise opens?
- Do they have any finance options?
- Do they an approved franchisor status with banks?
- Do they brokers that could assist with finance?
- Do they have vendor loan options?

4. How much working capital will I need to maintain to cover the franchise until it breaks even?

Aside from the initial startup costs, franchisees need enough operating capital for the first several months until the business breaks even, so it's important to find out the average amount of time it takes most franchisees to start turning a profit so that you can be financially prepared.

A financial modelling tool will assist with forecasting cashflow and required working capital.

Ask the franchisor:

- Do they have a debt-to-equity ratio (requirement of cash versus borrowings)?
- What is the break-even point?
- Do they help you determine the break-even point, or do they have a tool to do so?
- What are the best and worst-case scenarios that they have experienced with a franchisee in getting to the break-even point?
- How will they help you get to the break-even point?
- What examples can they share around how they have helped new franchisees get to the break-even?

5. What are the ongoing fees? How do your royalties and marketing fees work?

Take the time to understand your ongoing financial obligations to the franchisor, including whether you are obligated to pay royalty or other ongoing fees, such as for advertising. Understanding this is essential for managing the financial health of your business.

Ask the franchisor:

- What are the services that they provide on an ongoing basis as part of the royalties?
- How is the marketing fund administered?
- What can you expect from the marketing team and marketing fund?
- What is the status of the marketing fund (surplus or deficit)
- Are there any other fees I need to be aware of (remedial training, marketing support etc)?
- How do they determine the fees payable (POS, CRM etc.)?
    - Do you have to submit a sales report?
    - Do you get an invoice before fees are paid?
- How are the fees paid to the franchisor (direct debit, invoice, EFT)?
- What happens if I can't pay my franchise royalties and other fees?
- What are the financial implications of exiting the franchise before the end of the term?

6. How financially strong is the franchise company?

A franchisor has to provide the franchise entity's financial performance as an audited set of accounts each financial year after the franchisor has been trading for more than two completed financial years. For newer franchisors, they simply have to include a letter from an independent auditor stating that the business can meet its obligations as they fall due.

The established franchisor's audited financial statements can give you an indication of the franchise system's financial picture. Ask the franchisor to explain how they have shown steady growth and about their future — how the franchisor designates an adequate amount of funds to the system plans for growth. You'll also want to explore whether the bulk of their income comes from royalties or the sale of franchises and the questions listed below.

Ask the franchisor:

- How do they invest in the development of the franchise system?
- What initiatives are they working on at the moment to improve the franchise system?
- If you have access to their financial performance, ask them to provide a summary of the franchisor's financial performance, expenditure and any anomalies.

7. How many other locations are there, and what their your success rate?

The number of units a franchisor has determines their size but not necessarily their success. Are the franchisees receiving ample support? A large franchisor may be spread too thin, while an up-and-coming franchisor may not have enough resources. Ask what the success rate is among their franchisees and what the reasons are for failed units.

- What is the ratio of field support and head office support personnel to franchisees?
    - What are the plans for additional support personnel?

    - How do you access support from head office support departments?
- What is the development plan for the business?
    - Has the franchisor completed research and territory mapping?
    - What are the criteria for the success of a new territory/store/franchise?
    - How many locations will open each year?
    - What is the history of the growth of the network?
    - Does the business have a development/leasing/recruitment manager?
- How many franchises have closed?
    - Why did they close?
    - Discuss the franchisees that have left the franchise (details are in the disclosure document) and why did they leave?

8. How much money can I make?

Though a franchisor can't predict your individual success, they should have a good idea about what a typical franchisee earns and your income potential. Franchisors are unable to share some information with you and certainly cannot represent what the business you are entering into may do in terms of sales and profitability. This is coined a representation, and that may get them in trouble in the event of any legal proceedings.

It's worth asking this question to see how the franchisor responds.

Ask the franchisor:

- Does the franchisor have a financial modelling tool to assist you in evaluating the opportunity?

- Is the franchisor large enough to include the performance of the existing network in the FDD? (This is a requirement in the USA.)
- Can the franchisor share the performance of their company-operated units? (Some franchisors will share the performance quartiles of their franchisees.)
- You need to understand the average COGs, labour cost and rent as these are the three highest cost areas of operating a business.
- What is the expected or average return on capital, and how does this compare to the industry and sector average? (See examples in chapter 9).

9. What sets you apart from your competitors?

While the market for some brands is highly competitive and saturated, others are more innovative and unique, so it's important to understand the point of difference between operators. Observe with interest how the franchisor responds to the commentary on their competitors; hopefully, they are not critical of the competitor.

Ask the franchisor:

- Where does the brand fall sit on a competitive matrix?
- How is the brand positioned (branding, pricing, quality etc.)?
- What is the level of competition in the market, and who are the top competitors?
- Ask the franchisor about their unique selling points and their advantages over the competition.
- What value do they bring to customers?
- How does the business perform financially in comparison to competitors?

- What is the investment level?
- What are franchise fees and ongoing royalties?
- What is the return on capital?

10. What support do you offer beyond the initial training?

Most franchisors offer initial training to get your business up and running, but you'll want to find out what kind of ongoing support is available and how it compares to what similar franchisors offer.

Ask the franchisor:

- Ask to see the training materials (operations manual, SOPs, training manual)
  - Are they professional and comprehensive?
  - Are they online for easy access for team members?
  - How is franchisees and team members' proficiency verified?
- What support staff will be accessible to you on a day-to-day basis?
  - How often will you see my field support team?
  - What do they do when they visit or spend time with you?
- Are there ongoing training opportunities?
  - Is there a cost for any additional training?
- Is on-site assistance available?
- How often are franchise meetings held (video, conventions, training courses, state meetings)?
- What expertise does the franchisor have, and how will they support you as a franchisee? Consider the following aspects:
  - Marketing support
  - Operations and in-store support
  - Supply chain and competitive supply arrangements

    - Business profitability.

Make sure you feel comfortable with the level of support that will be available to you after you open your doors.

11. How do you resolve disagreements or disputes?

An important part of due diligence is investigating the franchisor's litigation history. The FDD discloses information regarding legal action involving the franchisor and its officers. In Australia, the Franchise Code of Conduct prescribes the legal process for dispute resolution, issuance of breach notices and termination.

Ask the franchisor:

- What is the process for handling disputes with franchisees?
- If the franchisor has any disputes recorded in the FDD, ask them about the details of that situation.
- Has the franchisor had any incidents of mediation or conciliation?
    - What was the outcome of those hearings?
- How do franchisees get into a disagreement with the franchisor?
    - How can a franchisee eliminate the potential for a dispute?
- Under what circumstances could the franchise agreement be terminated?
    - Can the franchisee sell the franchise in the event of a termination?
    - How is the franchisee protected from an unfair termination?

12. What are your expectations of your franchise owners?

As a franchisee, there are many expectations placed on you regarding payments, operations and other obligations per the franchise agreement.

It's important to have a discussion with the franchisor to gain a clear understanding surrounding what is required of you as a unit operator.

- What participation levels are expected of the franchisee?
    - Number of hours working in the business
    - Attendance at franchisor events
- What are the trading hours?
- Recommended pricing — is there a minimum, maximum?
    - Can the franchisee set their own pricing?
- What are the local area marketing expectations of the franchisee?
- What makes a good franchisee?

13. What will my territory be, and how will it be protected?

Learn how the franchisor manages territories for its franchisees and what rights you have under the agreement. The last thing you want to see happen is you opening a franchise only to have the franchisor open another business that impacts on your trade. You need to ask questions about the franchisor's development plan and how they determine where they open new franchises.

Ask the franchisor:

- Does the franchisor have territory mapping completed, which outlines the criteria for a territory?
    - Can you see the territories that are sold and available?
    - How do available territories or the site you are considering compare to the best-performing territories in the network?
- Do you get the territory and ability to open multiple locations within that territory?
    - Is there an additional fee to open another unit within the territory you own?

- Does the franchisor reserve the right to approve the location of your franchise?
- Will you have an exclusive or protected territory?
    - Is it an exclusive marketing territory or an exclusive territory?
- Will you have first right of refusal on a territory that may impact your existing territory?
- Can franchisees from outside your territory provide products or services within your territory?
- Will the franchisor have the ability to provide products or services within your territory?
- How will the franchisor police the franchisees' rights from another franchisee trading in the franchisee's territory?

Knowing whether you will be protected from competing units can have an impact on your success.

14. What kind of input will I have in marketing and advertising?
You will likely be obligated to contribute to a local, regional and/or national advertising fund as part of your agreement. Usually, marketing funds focus on growing the brand, but there are some direct benefits to franchisees, so it's important to understand how the fund is managed and what you can expect from the fund and marketing team and what requirements there are for local area marketing.

Ask the franchisor:

- What involvement do franchisees have in the use of marketing funds?
    - Is there a marketing committee made up of franchisees?

    - Are any of the funds used for targeted local marketing activities?
- Is there a marketing manual?
    - Is there a toolbox of ideas for local area marketing?
    - Are there POS and promotional marketing collateral templates available for franchisees to access?
- Is there a customer database and method for marketing to customers?
    - Is there a loyalty program?
    - What happens with online enquiries?
        - How are those enquiries managed, and do franchisees receive leads from these enquiries?
- Who manages the social media platforms?
    - Can the franchisee have their own social media accounts?
- Does the franchisee have to spend a certain amount of money on local area marketing?

15. What is a typical day like for a franchisee?

Learning about the day-to-day tasks and goals of a typical franchisee can help you get a clear picture of your daily work life. In addition, it's important to ask about the greatest challenges most franchisees face to help you decide whether the franchise opportunity will be a good fit for you.

Ask the franchisor:

- Does the franchisee have to complete the initial training?
- Does the franchisee have to work in the business?
    - How many hours does a franchisee have to spend in the business?
    - How many hours do other franchisees spend in the business?

- Can the franchisee have a manager to run the day-to-day operations?
  - If the franchisee has multiple locations, what is the expectation of the franchisor for the franchisee?

16. Can you speak with current franchisees about their experience?

This is a critical part of the due diligence investigation. Franchisors are required to disclose the contact information for both current and past franchisees. Speaking with both can give you an honest perspective on how the franchise system operates and its pros and cons. Be very cautious of any franchisor who tries to discourage you from reaching out to other operators.

Every franchise is different, and it's important to know exactly what you're buying into. A thorough investigation should cover all aspects of the franchise system and include information from the franchisor, past and present franchisees, and third-party sources. Some franchisors will have the validation part of the discovery process structured and won't want some prospective franchisees talking with existing franchisees if they are not far enough along the recruitment process,s as it may be an interruption to the existing franchisees' business.

Ask the franchisor:

- When can I speak with existing franchisees?
- What do you expect that I might hear when I talk to existing franchisees?
- Are you able to point me in the direction of the different types of franchisees to speak with (low/mid/high sales) top performing and underperforming franchisees?

- Do you have a list of questions that I am allowed or not allowed to ask?

Questions to Ask When Interviewing Franchisees

Prior to Investing in a Franchise, Interview Existing Franchisees

One of the most important steps in your journey to find the ideal franchise opportunity is what's known as validation. Validation refers to the process of interviewing franchisees who have bought into a concept that you have expressed interest in. It is during the validation process that you gain the most insight into whether a particular franchise opportunity is right for you.

The FDDs contain a list of every franchisee and, in most cases, contact information. You may choose to ask the franchisor for assistance in finding franchisees to speak to. However, it is strongly recommended that you seek out franchisees on your own.

The key to getting the most out of your conversation is to prepare a list of questions. In doing so, identify your goals. Is it important to learn about the day-to-day routine? About the experience with employees or customers? Perhaps understanding the role of the franchisor is necessary in helping you make a decision. These franchisees are busy, and you must be respectful of their time. You may not get all of your questions answered, so it is important to prioritise them.

Every franchise system will have a range of franchisees, High performers, those struggling and everything in between. Work to speak to franchisees that represent each section of the group. If you encounter a franchisee that is negative, perhaps explore that line of questioning with other franchisees to determine if it is a systemic problem or particular to that franchisee. Some people (franchisees) are just different (glass-half-full and those that are glass-half-empty), so try to see beyond the individual and focus on the specific issue rather than how the individual feels about it. Every franchise system will have franchisees that are negative and those that are positive so focus on the business not the people. The more franchisees you speak with, the better a snapshot you will have.

Top 10 Questions to Ask When Interviewing Franchisees:

1. **What has been the most rewarding part of being a franchisee? What has been the most unexpected struggle?**

How the franchisee responds to these questions will tell you a great deal about how closely expectations have been met.

2. **What were you doing prior to being a franchisee?**

Understanding a franchisee's background may offer insight into what personality type and what skill set aligns with the franchise opportunity.

3. **Was the training and assistance in opening your location provided by the franchisor adequate? What could they have done better?**

One of the biggest benefits of buying a franchise is not doing it alone. For a good system, that starts before you are open for business. Ask the franchisee how prepared they felt once open and if there is anything they think should be added to the training.

4. How has the franchisor's support been since you have been open for business? You want to know what the operational support is like but also how do they help with the changing face of business (labour costs, supply chain and COGs)

Most franchisors assign an employee, typically titled an area manager/business or operations consultant, to your location to periodically check in. This person's job is twofold. One, to assist you with day-to-day operations, and two, to ensure you are abiding by the guidelines set forth by the franchisor. Ask the franchisee what kind of assistance he or she has provided. How often do they make a visit? All-in-all, does the franchisee feel properly supported? Does the franchisor have support staff with expertise to assist you in managing the costs of operating a business?

5. Is the franchisor accessible when you need them to be?

The area manager/business or operations consultant assistance comes with limitations, and so, someone from corporate will have to be contacted when concerns need to be escalated. Ask the franchisee what issues have arisen that led to them reaching out to a senior member of the franchisor team. Were they happy with the attention paid to their concern and its resolution? The last thing anyone wants is to feel as if their investment is not important to anyone outside of the corporate offices.

6. How many hours a week do you work? Is that more, less or about the same as you expected?

Many who become business owners do so because they want the flexibility that comes with owning your own business. Yet that doesn't happen on day one. Most franchisees work a good number of hours in the first few years. Ask the franchisee if they feel the investment has provided a better work–life balance. If the answer is 'no', do they see that happening soon?

7. What assistance does the franchisor provide with marketing?

Franchisees bring a lot of skill to the table. Perhaps they have a strong sales or management background or experience in the field the franchisor concept specialises in. What many don't have experience in is the marketing piece. All the grit and talent in the world won't mean anything if you can't drive traffic through your doors. Franchisors know this and work hard to help franchisees overcome it. Most have a designated marketing department that focuses on both national exposure and local-level marketing. Ask the franchisee if they are getting their money's worth with regard to their contributions to the marketing fund. What local marketing efforts do they provide guidance with? How important is social media, and what tools do they recommend franchisees use?

8. Are you happy with the financial returns to date? Do you feel you are on your way to meeting all of your financial goals?

Your gut says to start out the conversation with 'How much do you make?' Don't. That's a very personal question, and one many franchisees may not be comfortable answering. Simply finding out how happy the franchisee is with their financial performance will say a great deal. If they are not happy, what do they attribute that to? Do they see themselves overcoming current challenges and ultimately hitting their goals? Who knows, you may find a franchisee or two who is very open with their financials and willing to share any and all details. However, you won't find such a franchisee if one of the first questions you ask is about money. Establish a rapport first. Make sure this question comes later in your conversation.

9. Do you have any advice for me as I continue with the exploration process?

What does the franchisee wish they did differently while doing their due diligence? Is there a question they wished they asked? Is there information they found out later that they felt was important to know before signing their agreement?

10. If you had to do it all over, would you make the investment again?

Just as with question no. 1, how the franchisee answers this question is very telling of their overall experience.

CHAPTER 14

THE TOP 10 TIPS

These Are the Musts for the Franchise that You're Considering Getting into

Top 10 Traits of Successful Franchisors

1. A proven business model

The business needs to deliver a fair ROI that is as competitive or more competitive than other comparable franchise opportunities. The business needs to have traded and demonstrated success, ideally across multiple locations.

The size of the network or the age of the business does provide a longer history to demonstrate the proof of concept, but this does not mean a smaller, younger brand may not be a good opportunity; both should be able to demonstrate their financial performance.

Does the franchisor make available to you the evidence of the financial performance of the network?

2. A dedicated, involved and well-supported

The more help you can get from a franchisor, in most cases, the better your chances of success. The franchisor has built a successful business and knows how to run things to be profitable, but they need to be able to demonstrate that they have and will support you as a franchisee.

Does the franchisor have the right quality and number of support personnel to assist you in your business?

3. A strong, recognisable brand

The brand needs to have recognition and a loyal customer following. It is important that the brand understands who their target customer is and that they market to them on the platforms that are appropriate to that audience.

The franchisor needs to invest in marketing and have the right resources in place to help you market the brand within your territory.

4. Happy and successful franchisees

The true test of a franchise system is the satisfaction and success of existing franchisees, and this is why it is so important to conduct franchise interviews as part of your discovery process.

Doing good validation will inform you of the franchisor's past performance, which may indicate future performance for you as a franchisee.

5. Competition

It's important to understand the competitive landscape: who are the competitors and how is the franchise that you are considering differentiated from those competitors? When considering location, research needs to be done regarding just how competitive the territory is. If the territory is saturated, it may be difficult to change consumer habits and have them come to your business.

6. An excellent location

When it comes to real estate, we've all heard of the catch call 'Location, location, location'. Never is this more relevant than a business that relies on customers coming onto the premise. For a business that sells to the public, like a retail outlet or restaurant, an excellent location is a busy strip mall or shopping precinct with signage visible from the main road and lots throughout traffic. A business park with lots of offices may be another great place for a restaurant franchise.

For mobile franchises or others that don't require customers to come to them, an excellent location may still provide visibility of signage or may have low rent even though it's in a safe, clean area of town.

7. Flexibility to change

As we've seen during the pandemic of 2020, businesses need to have the ability to adjust their business model and pivot in times of change. Franchisees need a franchisor that is constantly looking to evolve and innovate.

Things people must have, even during bad economic times, are usually profitable, such as grocery stores, budget restaurants and retail stores known for their low prices.

8. Freedom from legal entanglements

It's worth a little research to make sure there is no pending litigation or even convictions against the franchisor that may impact on the franchisors' profitability or focus on the business. It may also indicate the strength of management and approach with franchisees.

9. Right price

This does not necessarily mean inexpensive. A franchise with great profit potential will likely cost more than others but will also offer a greater return. Don't be afraid to pay more if the franchise will yield a greater profit. It is worth asking the franchisor what the resale values have been on previous sales. It is important to know if the EBITDA multiple is at or above the industry average.

The second part of pricing relates to positioning in the market because different areas will have different sensitivities based on demographics. Fast-food restaurants have done well in tough economic periods, as have luxury retailers. It's the middle market that has found a challenge during periods of recession and fiscal tightening.

10. Confidence

There are two types of confidence that you are looking for: the confidence that the franchisor instils in you throughout the recruitment process and the confidence that existing franchisees have in the network.

But the most important aspect is the confidence that you have in your decision-making about the franchise opportunity. This is a combination of the research that you need to complete to evaluate the opportunity and your gut feeling. If it doesn't feel right, don't do it.

Top 10 Traits of Successful Franchisees

1. Leadership and communication

Successful franchisees are typically successful leaders. A great leader is influential, with good decision-making and, most importantly, excellent communication skills which are necessary for leading and motivating staff as well as ensuring that the franchise provides impressive customer service.

The franchisee needs to be a leader in their category and be an effective communicator with their target audience both in person and from a marketing perspective.

2. Risk-taking

Though the implied risks of starting a business are reduced with a franchise versus a startup, there are some inherent risks that come with investing in a franchise. A great franchisee should be comfortable with taking the chance on a franchise being successful as well as be able to take calculated risks that will help make their business grow.

Remember, in chapter 4, we discussed the difference between the risk-seeker and the risk-tolerator. Business is a risk, but it needs to be a calculated risk. With risk comes reward, and often, the bigger the risk, the bigger the reward.

3. Willingness to learn

There's not much room for ego in franchising — you need to be willing to learn and grow. It's important to understand that you will need to accept training and guidance from the franchisor. Every circumstance — positive or negative — should be viewed as a learning experience that can help you get to the next level and become even more profitable and successful.

4. Adaptability

Being adaptable is key as a franchisee. Possessing the ability to be flexible and adapt to changing circumstances is a must as well as being resilient and able to bounce back from missteps as you establish your new business.

5. Being thick-skinned

Like all kinds of business leaders, franchisees face a steady stream of advice and criticism daily. The ability to roll with the punches, persevere and take advice from others is critical. Being thick-skinned means not being easily offended by feedback from the franchisor, customers and employees alike.

6. Being a team player

Franchising is not an independent enterprise. Franchise agreements require you to follow a specific set of business practices established by the franchisor and used with success by other franchisees. Uniformity is necessary so that customers know what to expect at any franchise location. The ability to follow a system and play by the rules is not only expected of a franchisee but also required.

7. Financial aptitude

Running a franchise requires financial knowledge, including how to figure out profit and loss, labour and materials costs and do accounting for the business. Financial stability often needs to be demonstrated before you can purchase a franchise. Successful franchisees have a propensity for handling finances both personally and business-wise.

8. Patience

Rome wasn't built in a day, and your franchise won't be built in a day, a month, or possibly even a year. It can take time to see success; meanwhile, long hours and a lot of sweat equity will be the norm. A franchisee who can keep expectations realistic will have an advantage over others who may not be patient enough to keep making an effort long enough to see profits and success.

9. Being results driven

Although you receive help from the franchisor, your success as a franchisee is ultimately up to you. Successful franchisees are driven by setting and obtaining measurable goals to stay focused and on track towards making the franchise a success.

10. Passion

Without the passion and drive for success, it is unlikely that you will be successful. Likewise, a passion for your brand will be very evident to your customers and will be contagious as well. A franchisee with a passion for success and for the product or services they are selling will go above and beyond to make sure their business is successful.

In Summary

Both parties, franchisee and franchisor, have a role to play in the success of the franchise business and business failure can be boiled down to two things — being lazy and stupid!

Now that may seem harsh, but to invest so substantially themselves and their money — and to then not use what they've bought/created or not to do the work — is both LAZY and STUPID!

Lazy

- If the franchise owner does not work smart and hard.
- If the franchisor does not constantly innovate and improve the system and business model.

Stupid

- If the franchise owner fails to use the proven system correctly!
- If the franchisor fails to support their franchisees
- Franchising works; the franchisor has proven the model to be successful, they've invested time, money and expertise to get their business franchisable. The franchisee needs to make the same investment, that's why everyone needs to be invested.